CAPT Writing Across the Disciplines

Sharon Shirley
Branford High School
Branford, CT

Kate Mullan
Windsor High School
Windsor, CT

Contributing Editors
Sara Fucci
Bethel High School
Bethel, CT

Gary Lawlor
Bethel High School
Bethel, CT

Melissa Mirabello
Berlin High School
Berlin, CT

Cynthia Morrill
Putnam High School
Putnam, CT

*A **Get Smart Book**® from*

WEBSTER HOUSE

PUBLISHING LLC

Ridgefield, Connecticut

Cover Art: The Great American Art Company, Inc.
Book Design and Typography: 1106 Design

Library of Congress Control Number: 2004100350

ISBN: 1-932635-02-5

Printed in the United States of America

10 9 8 7 6 5 4 3 2 1

For additional information about Webster House Publishing LLC titles or "Get Smart Book"® titles, contact us on the Internet at *http://www.websterhousepub.com*, or write to Webster House Publishing LLC, Box 294, Georgetown, CT 06829.

Table of Contents

Foreword

I was very lucky to have excellent grammar teachers throughout my schooling. My high school teachers in particular, Mrs. Peters and Mrs. Wilson, worked very hard to ensure that each of their students had a firm grasp on the rules of grammar, and that we knew how to use them to edit our work effectively and efficiently. Without their help, I never would have been able to be as successful as I was in college and my work careers, or to write this book as quickly and as accurately as I have.

However, in order to ensure that I gave you proper, up-to-date (yes, the accepted rules of our language do change), and thorough guidance, I referred to several sources throughout my writing process. Instead of merely putting them in a bibliography, I am including them in the Appendix. They are great resources on the rules of grammar, and many of them offer several additional examples to help you in your understanding. Some of the sites also provide quizzes so you can test your mastery of the skills. If you cannot find what you need on one of the Internet sites in the Appendix, there are numerous other sites available with similar information. You can find them easily by using any reputable search engine. As you prepare for CAPT, and when you have questions about the correct rules when you are writing papers, use these sites to help you.

—Sharon Shirley

Chapter 1:
The CAPT–What Is It?

Test-taking is rarely fun, and, if we had our choice, most of us would rather use the paper to make paper airplanes than take a test. Yet, Connecticut state and federal laws require public schools to provide evidence that they are offering students appropriate and sufficient instruction of knowledge and skills in several core areas. One of the ways to do this is to assess students on how well they can use these skills. In Connecticut, this assessment is done yearly through the Connecticut Mastery Test, given at the fourth-, sixth-, and eighth-grade levels; and the Connecticut Academic Performance Test (CAPT), which is given in the spring of the tenth grade. So, like it or not, you have one last required standardized test to take and pass before you graduate.

The CAPT is used to assess individual students' skills and knowledge and how well a school district is doing in preparing students for participation in the working world. In this regard, your scores tell you what skills you are mastering or need to improve. They also tell schools where to make adjustments in curriculum so that students are learning what they need to know in order to become successful and productive adults in today's world.

Thus, while you might not enjoy test-taking, it is an important part of your educational process. Assessments can help you understand what you have learned and show you where you need to work harder to improve your skills. The key areas that are tested by CAPT are mathematics, science, reading across the disciplines, and writing across the disciplines. The focus of this book is on the writing portion of the CAPT and the skills it assesses.

"Writing Across the Disciplines" and What the Test Shows About Your Skills

Writing is a primary form of communication in our society, especially so in today's world. Careers in all fields require that you be able to write effectively in order to make sure your readers can understand you. Additionally, as citizens in a democratic society, we use our writing skills on an everyday basis. Clear and effective writing helps you correct bank errors, express your interest in a proposed community program, or tell your senator why he or she should not vote to eliminate funding for a project you believe is important.

To be a successful writer, you need to learn how to write about a variety of topics as well as how to communicate with people in different disciplines. A discipline is a subject area, such as science, history, math, or English. A discipline can also be part of a larger subject area, such as history, politics, civics, or psychology, which are all grouped under the heading of social sciences. The writing portion of the CAPT is designed to assess how well you communicate across multiple disciplines.

Are You a Writer?

Every person is a writer. However, each individual has different skills. Some individuals are very talented with words, and can sit down and write a creative, funny story within an hour or two. Others struggle in that same amount of time to get just a few paragraphs on paper. No matter which category you fit into, you are a writer: Since kindergarten you have learned to use the English language to put your thoughts into written words. The CAPT Writing Across the Disciplines assessment is intended to show that you can express yourself in writing so that others can understand your meaning. It is intended for all writers, not merely those who are incredibly talented with words.

The Test's Format

There are two parts to the CAPT Writing Across the Disciplines assessment. In the Interdisciplinary Writing portion, you will be given three articles to read. These articles will focus on a topic from various disciplines, such as medicine, culture, or education. You will use information from the articles to write a *first draft* of a persuasive letter about that topic. In that letter you will take a position and support it with appropriate evidence from the reading and any prior knowledge you may have. You will do this two different times, on different topics, during the CAPT assessment period. Each piece of writing represents 35% of your Writing Across the Disciplines score.

In the second part of the CAPT Writing Across the Disciplines assessment, you will be tested on your revising and editing skills, which are important parts of the writing process. In this portion of the test, you revise writing samples to improve word choice, punctuation, and other mechanics in order to make a piece of writing more clear and readable. In this section, you will read three short selections and answer approximately 18 questions about how to make clearer what you just read. This part of the test is worth 30% of your Writing Across the Disciplines score.

Understanding the Readings

The Writing Across the Disciplines portion of the CAPT tests your writing and editing skills more so than your knowledge. That is, it tests what you are able *to do* more than it tests what facts and formulas you have acquired throughout your education. There are five key areas of skills that you will be assessed on in Writing Across the Disciplines. You have worked on developing and refining these skills over the last few years in school. They include:

1. Reading critically
2. Constructing an informed opinion
3. Organizing thoughts
4. Communicating opinions appropriately for a specific audience
5. Using standard English grammar and vocabulary

Following is a brief discussion of these skills. More advice about how to use them and how to demonstrate that you can use them on the CAPT is given later in this text.

Reading Critically

Reading critically means reading with an awareness of the perspective, or bias, the author may have. It also means that you question what the author is telling you, or not telling you, so that you look for the bigger picture and not just the narrow focus presented by the author. The readings in the CAPT were chosen carefully to allow you to identify reasons and evidence to support the position you choose to defend in your writing.

Constructing an Informed Opinion

How well can you construct an informed opinion? The writing portion of the CAPT will assess how well you can you take a position on an issue and defend it with specific reasoning and evidence. Having an opinion on a matter is much different from having an *informed* opinion. The key is to show that you can make rational arguments to support your point of view and convince others to agree with you.

Organizing Thoughts

While having an informed opinion is important, you also need to be able to organize your thoughts logically so that readers can follow your train of thought. To be a strong writer, it helps to establish your meaning if you organize the paragraphs within the document, as well as the sentences within each paragraph.

Communicating Opinions Appropriately for a Specific Audience

Understanding how to communicate your opinions with a particular audience is a specific skill you need to have. In this regard, your audience will impact the tone of your writing, the vocabulary you choose, and the manner in which you present your evidence. If you are writing to your state senator requesting that she vote to reduce the number of school days each year, you would likely use a respectful and formal tone. If you are writing a letter to the editor about the same topic, your tone, while still respectful, may not need to be as formal.

Using Standard English Grammar and Vocabulary

All the skills mentioned in this section will become more effective if you know how to use the English language correctly. Without proper grammar and word choice, what you intend to say in your writing might not be what the audience actually gets from reading it. The initial drafts of most writing generally do not focus intently on word choice, sentence length, or grammar. These changes are made in the revising and editing process. Since you will be writing your Interdisciplinary Writing pieces in such a short time period, you don't have much of an opportunity to review and revise for accuracy and clarity. Your responses to those sections will be assessed as drafts. Your grammar and usage generally are not assessed on your written responses to those two topics. However, in order to ensure that you are mastering the skills required to refine your writing, the Editing and Revising portion allows you to show that you understand the basic rules of the language.

If you are feeling a little overwhelmed at this point, that's okay. In writing, just as in most everything you do in life, there is a process in which you must follow a series of steps to make decisions for completing the task. Think about all the steps it takes to make a peanut butter sandwich. If you start with taking out the necessary tools and ingredients and then think about the actual steps you must take to successfully make the sandwich, the task may seem more complex than it really is. However, you know you can make a peanut butter sandwich quite easily, even though your brain must go through several steps in order to get from the thought of the sandwich to the actual sandwich itself. It is the same with taking the Writing Across the Disciplines test. You have been developing your thinking and writing skills for years, since you wrote your first paragraph and read your first short story. All you are doing now is refining these skills by reexamining the various steps involved so that you are equipped to prove you have a thorough understanding of each part of the process on the CAPT.

Scoring

CAPT scoring procedures are both rather simple and yet also very complicated. They are simple because they start with a basic score on each section of the test—the two Interdisciplinary Writing pieces, and the Editing and Revising portion. The Editing and Revising score is based on the number of items you answer correctly. If you answer 14 correctly, you get 14 points. Simple enough, right? The Interdisciplinary Writing score is a bit more detailed and confusing.

Each piece of the Interdisciplinary Writing is assessed holistically on a scale of 1–6 using the rubric shown in Figure 1.1. Holistic scoring means that your writing is graded "as a whole." The people who score your writing will read it carefully and judge it based on the factors in the rubric. You will receive the score for the criteria that most closely matches the writing you produced on the test. The scorers have been trained very thoroughly on how to determine which score category your writing, as a whole, is most like. Take a moment to read over the rubric to get a general idea of how your writing will be assessed. The rubric and its specific criteria will be explained later in greater detail.

Figure 1.1: Rubric for Interdisciplinary Writing Test

Score Point	Criteria
1	• May take a position and address the problem; little or no awareness of audience is shown. • The response offers little or no support from the source materials, OR the support provided is copied verbatim. • The support may be emotional, inaccurate, and irrelevant, or show serious misunderstanding. • The response lacks focus and a controlling idea; little or no organization is present, and frequent digressions and/or abrupt shifts in the response interfere with the meaning. • Many ideas are difficult to understand; fluency and transitions are lacking.
2	• May take a position and address the problem; little, if any, audience awareness is shown. • The response contains only superficial support and/or may use information from only one or two of the source materials. • The supporting ideas may be poorly developed and/or illogical and inconsistent; the information may be inaccurate or irrelevant. • The response may lack focus and a controlling idea; digressions and/or abrupt shifts in the response interfere with the meaning. • Some ideas may be difficult to understand; fluency and transitions are lacking.
3	• Takes a position, but the position may not be clearly developed; some awareness of audience may be shown. • The response contains limited support and may not use information from each of the source materials. • The supporting ideas are few and/or only somewhat developed; some information may be inaccurate or irrelevant. • The response is somewhat organized, but there may be digressions or abrupt shifts that interfere with meaning. • Some ideas may not be clearly expressed; fluency and transitions may be lacking.

Score Point	Criteria
4	• Takes and develops a position; some awareness of audience is shown, but persuasiveness may be lacking. • The response contains adequate support but may not use information from each of the source materials. • The supporting ideas are adequately but not thoroughly developed; some information may be inaccurate or irrelevant. • The response is adequately organized with at least one controlling idea; digressions, if present, are not disruptive. • Most ideas are clear and understandable, but fluency and transitions may be lacking.
5	• Takes a clear and persuasive position; awareness of audience is evident. • The position is well supported, typically using information from each of the source materials. • The supporting ideas are generally well developed; information is accurate and relevant. • The response is well organized and contains one or more controlling ideas; digressions are rare. • Most ideas are clearly expressed; writing is generally fluent, with some use of transitions.
6	• Takes a clear, thoughtful, and persuasive position; keen awareness of audience is shown. • The position is richly supported with information from each of the source materials. • The supporting ideas are very well developed; information is accurate and relevant. • The response is unified and focused and contains one or more controlling ideas; organization and control are sustained throughout the response. • The ideas are clearly and effectively developed; writing is fluent and polished with effective transitions.

Two people, who are called "readers," score each of your pieces of writing. The scores for the two readers are then added together to reach a score between 2 and 12 for each piece. Two points are then subtracted from each of those scores, and the new numbers are multiplied by 2.1. Those new numbers are then added together, along with the number of correct responses you gave to the Revising and Editing portion of the test to come up with what is called a "Composite Raw Score." This score will range from 0 to 60 points. See Figure 1.2 for an example.

Figure 1.2: Sample Score Calculation

Example:

Test 1
Score from Reader 1 = 5
Score from Reader 2 = 5

Test 1: $10 - 2 = 8$
$8 \times 2.1 = 16.8$

Test 2
Score from Reader 1 = 4
Score from Reader 2 = 5

Test 2: $9 - 2 = 7$
$7 \times 2.1 = 14.7$

Interdisciplinary Writing Score = $16.8 + 14.7 = 31.5$
$+ 16$ (Revising and Editing Score)

$47.5 = $ Composite Raw Score

A "raw score" is a number that is usually based only on the number of items you answer correctly on an exam. In this case, however, it is based on two holistic scores and one objective score (the Editing and Revising score). It still represents a "raw score" because it is the score you earned on this test.

The Composite Raw Score is then converted into another score by using a scale that is established to rank your performance on the test into one of four levels. The scale is also based on the comparison of the relative complexity of the test you take to the tests taken by students in other years. This is done in case the form of the test you took was easier or harder than the forms given in previous years. Your score is converted on a table to another number, which is then used to determine whether you have reached the level 1, 2, 3, or 4 band (see figure 1.3) on your writing skills.

Score Bands

The score bands of 1–4 have very general meanings. A score in the 4 band means that you have met the "goal" for what the state of Connecticut expects of a student completing his or her tenth-grade year. A score in band 3 means that you are proficient—you can do what you need to do to communicate in writing using the English language but you could probably do so a little better with a little more work. A score in bands 1 and 2 is cause for concern. Either you experienced a poor testing day, or you are really struggling with writing. A score in either of those bands is a cue to your parents and your teachers that you need some extra help in developing your writing skills.

Figure 1.3

Score Band	Meaning
4	**Goal**—You are performing at the skill level standard set by the state of Connecticut.
3	**Proficient**—You are competent in the skills, but you still have work to do to refine them.
2	**Basic**—You have a grasp of the skills, but have not fully developed them.
1	**Below Basic**—You need to work on the skills.

What Is a Good Score?

Connecticut has recently passed legislation to require schools to make CAPT test scores and/or similar assessments graduation requirements for students. Therefore, you need to do your very best so that you can get a diploma from your school when you graduate. However, as I always advise my students, do the best you can on the test with the circumstances in which you find yourself on the day of the test. For instance, if you are suffering from a cold on the day of one of the tests, you might not perform as well as you would if you were feeling well. By reading this book, working through the examples and the practice tests, and working with your parents and your teachers to reinforce and refine your skills, you will improve your chances to meet the state's goal on the writing portion of the CAPT.

Chapter 2:
Writing Is a Process

We tend to think that if we are armed with an idea and a pen, we are ready to write. However, writing is much more complex. While the pen and idea are important, we need to equip ourselves with much more in order to produce our best work. The writer's arsenal includes many skills that are used in one or more of the stages of writing: brainstorming, planning, drafting, revising, editing, and finalizing.

You have probably studied each of these steps in detail over the last several years of school. Here is a brief summary of them to refresh your memory.

- **Brainstorming** is just what it sounds like: stirring up the thoughts in your brain just as a rainstorm might stir up the leaves on your lawn. During the brainstorming stage, you jot down all your ideas connected in any way to what you might write about, whether they make complete sense at the time or not. You might use graphic organizers such as charts, Venn Diagrams, webs, or other visuals to help you in this process. This stage is not the time to rule out any of your thoughts—you never know what might be the next source of your inspiration.

- **Planning** is the next stage. You choose your central ideas from your brainstorming, and you plan out a route to follow, from introducing your idea to your reader to wrapping it up at the end. Some people prefer to write a detailed outline, while others simply jot down three or four ideas and work with the details as they go. The key, as with much of life, is to do what works best for you. While you may stray from the original outline, planning gives you a general direction so that you can start getting your words and thoughts from your brainstorming session down on paper.

- **Drafting** your writing may be the hardest stage, because you are making the first attempt at putting your ideas together in a fluent, organized, and comprehensive manner. During this stage, your focus should be getting your notes and ideas from the brainstorming and planning stages into different paragraphs, with an introduction and a conclusion. Oftentimes, we struggle over how to say something perfectly the first time. Other times, we try to revise and reorganize as we write our first draft. During the drafting stage, however, focus on getting the ideas out of your mind and into coherent words. You can fix problem areas, such as wordiness or lack of clarity, and jazz it up with specific terminology and fancy sentence structure in the next stage.

- **Revising** your draft may seem difficult because like most writers, you may tend to attach yourself to what you create, and it can be tough to make changes to your own work. However, revising work helps to make it better. Moving a paragraph from one place to another may make it more meaningful and enhance the point you are trying to make. Using more effective vocabulary and varying your sentence structure can make your writing more engaging. At this stage, you can also determine whether all the details you used are relevant to what you are trying to convey to your reader and whether all the information you included is necessary to your piece of work. You should also focus on refining your transitions between sentences and paragraphs at this stage.

- **Editing** for mechanics—that is, grammar, spelling, and punctuation—follows the revision stage. After you have made your changes, you need to read your new draft to make sure you have stayed true to the rules of the English language. At this point you need to fix any errors, double check your use of punctuation, and make sure you have spelled all those tricky words correctly.

- **Finalizing** your writing is the point in the process where you produce the piece in a publishable form—to submit to your teacher or your boss, or to mail to your mayor or bank president. This final version of your writing is in as perfect form as possible considering your subject matter, tone, audience, intent, and use of the language. At this stage, you should be able to look at what you have accomplished and take pride in the work you have done.

Two aspects of writing should be on your mind throughout each of the stages: audience and purpose, both of which affect your tone. For whom are you writing, and what is it that you want them to get out of it? If you are writing a children's story, you will likely choose different words and simpler sentence structures than if you are writing to a scientist to request information. If you are asking someone to do something for you, your tone will take on a different aspect than if you are telling a story about an exciting event you witnessed. As you brainstorm, plan, draft, and revise, you should be paying special attention to your tone with respect to your audience and purpose.

As you consider this information and think about the writing you have done in the past, you have probably realized that writing takes time. Ideally, it is not wise to set a specific, limited time period to produce a written work to the best of your ability. Very often, the writing process can take days, weeks, or even months.

So, you might ask, why does the state test how well you write if you are not allowed the time it takes to follow a comprehensive writing process? The CAPT has two parts so that you are tested on the different stages of the process under different circumstances. Is it a true test of how well you can write if given the chance to go through the stages properly? Probably not, but it gives you a fair chance to show that you can write with a certain degree of skill.

The Writing Process and the CAPT

Interdisciplinary Writing: Brainstorming through Drafting

The Interdisciplinary Writing section of CAPT focuses on the earlier stages of the writing process: it gives you a topic, narrows your purpose, and informs you of your audience. The test also gives you background information on which to develop your ideas. On this part of the test you will show that you can gather ideas (brainstorm), put your ideas in logical order (plan), and then write your ideas in paragraph form (draft). Your work then is assessed as a *first draft*—it does not have to be perfect. The assessors look for evidence that you have mastered certain skills—such as taking and supporting a position and organizing your thoughts—that are set forth on the rubric, which are discussed in Chapter 3.

Interdisciplinary Writing: Editing and Revising

In the Editing and Revising portion of the CAPT Writing Across the Disciplines component, you will demonstrate your skills at reorganizing sentences and sentence structure, choosing appropriate vocabulary, and making corrections to grammar and other mechanics so that you can improve a piece of writing. In consideration of time constraints, the state provides you with three pieces of writing and several multiple-choice questions. The questions ask you to select the best answer to improve the writing. The specific skills they assess are discussed in Chapters 7 and 8.

Getting Help with the Writing Process

This chapter gives you an overview of the writing process in general. It assumes that you have been acquainted with it and used it often in your educational career. The steps in the process are detailed in later chapters. However, if you are struggling with any of the steps of the writing process, seek out a teacher, current or past, who has challenged you in your writing. Ask that person if he or she can help you with the stages of the process that are the most difficult for you. There are also many sources on the writing process that can help you. Some of these are listed at the end of the text in the Appendix. Most important, do not give up; do not consider yourself a "nonwriter"; and keep working at it. Just as practice on the ball field helps you improve your throw, practice with words will help you improve your writing.

Chapter 3:
Interdisciplinary Writing Test–The Skills

The Interdisciplinary Writing Test assesses your skill level in six basic areas:

1. Taking a position
2. Comprehensiveness
3. Supporting your argument
4. Organization
5. Clarity and fluency

The rubric is geared directly toward these skills, and the people who assess your writing are focused on how well you do all these as a whole. Throughout this chapter, you can explore each of these skills in general terms through examining what they are and how you can demonstrate them. Chapter 4 focuses on how they are specifically incorporated into the CAPT Interdisciplinary Writing test.

Taking a Position

One of the skills the CAPT assesses is how well you can take a position on an issue and argue for or against it clearly and appropriately to your reader. You need to show that you can review an issue and use logical reasoning to support a side. You want to be able to convince the reader that you truly understand the issue, that your position is the correct one, and that he or she should take the action you recommend.

When you take a position and write about it, it is important that you are very clear in your wording so that there is no doubt which side you are arguing. *Above all, be sure to choose a side; waffling from one side to the other will most likely result in a failing score.* You should choose words that show you are so convinced of your viewpoint that the people who argue the other side cannot make a stronger argument. To do this, you need to be aware of your audience so that the tone, background information, and reasoning you use are appropriate. You also need to be persuasive, using words that are convincing and arguments that make sense.

If you take a look at the rubric for the Interdisciplinary Writing, you will note that the first item at each score point level addresses how well you take a position. The figure below identifies the criteria for you.

Figure 3.1: Score Criteria for Taking a Position

Score Point	Criteria
1	May take a position and address the problem; little or no awareness of audience is shown.
2	May take a position and address the problem; little, if any, audience awareness is shown.
3	Takes a position, but the position may not be clearly developed; some awareness of audience may be shown.
4	Takes and develops a position; some awareness of audience is shown, but persuasiveness may be lacking.
5	Takes a clear and persuasive position; awareness of audience is evident.
6	Takes a clear, thoughtful, and persuasive position; keen awareness of audience is shown.

Take a couple of minutes to read over the criteria at each level. Highlight the descriptive words that seem to be the key for determining how well you score. Jot down what it is that the assessors are looking for among each level. In doing so, consider the following:

- How do the criteria for a score of 3 differ from the criteria for a score of 1 or 2?
- What is the biggest difference between the criteria for a score of 3 and the criteria for a score of 4?
- What do you need to do to raise your score from 4 to 5 or 6?

You will note that your writing is assessed at a higher score level on this aspect if it is clear and persuasive, and proves awareness of your audience.

Examples for Taking a Position

Read the following three paragraphs and try to assess where they would fall on the rubric under the "Taking a Position" skill. Each example is based on an assignment to write to the town commission about installing traffic lights at an intersection that has had an increase in traffic. Jot down some notes as you read the paragraphs and compare your ideas to the criteria for this skill. Here are some questions to consider as you read each example:

1. To what extent does the example take a clear position? Why?
2. How persuasive is the example? Why?
3. How does the example show an awareness of the audience?
4. Which example would probably receive a 1 or 2 on the rubric? Why?
5. Which example would likely receive a 3 or 4 on the rubric? Why?
6. Which example would be the most likely to get a 5 or 6 on the rubric? Why?

Example 1

The stop signs at the corner of Burke and Main need to be removed and replaced with traffic lights because there have been too many accidents at that intersection (four in the last month). Many people fail to make a complete stop at that intersection, and others get too confused about when they have the right of way. There are also a great many pedestrians who use that intersection, and stoplights with crosswalk lights will make it safer for them. Please consider the safety of pedestrians and drivers who use that intersection and vote to have the stoplights installed.

Example 2

The intersection of Burke Street and Main Street is very crowded. Yesterday, I had to wait about five minutes to cross it with my bicycle. My friend rode across right away, but that probably was not a smart thing to do because people are not careful there. Sometimes they do not even stop at the stop signs. But sometimes it's good to not have a traffic light there because you don't have to wait for a green light when there is no other traffic. Something needs to be done to make it safer and less of a problem.

Example 3

You have to change the traffic rules at the intersection of Burke and Main because a great many people have been hurt there lately. There should be some changes made, such as removing the stop signs and putting in traffic lights. Drivers and pedestrians will be safer that way, and there will be fewer accidents.

Analysis of Examples

The examples above can be analyzed using the following chart (Figure 3.2), which examines each example for how clearly it takes a position, persuades the reader, and shows awareness of audience. Read the chart across for each aspect of this skill assessment and down for how well each example succeeds at showing the aspect. Take a few moments to study the chart and compare it to the notes you made while you were reading the examples.

Figure 3.2: Analysis of Examples

Aspect	Example	Extent of Success	Support
Takes a clear position?	1	Strong	Clearly states that traffic lights should replace the stop signs and provides reasons.
	2	Weak	Acknowledges the problem, but does not really take a position on what should be done, if anything.
	3	Medium	Takes a position, but does not provide specific information as to why the change should be made.
Is persuasive?	1	Strong	Uses persuasive words, e.g., must, safety; does not waver; focus is on the issue.
	2	Weak	Does not convince the reader to do anything in particular.
	3	Medium	Wording could be stronger (i.e., should); suggests alternative but seems uncertain (i.e., such as).
Shows awareness of audience?	1	Strong	Clearly asks the reader in a respectful tone to vote to make the specific change.
	2	Weak	Does not show that the writer knows how the reader can help; informal tone does not show as much respect for the reader as it could.
	3	Medium	Shows some knowledge about reader's role to make change, but not in a specific way.

Example 1 would probably earn the higher score because it clearly takes the position that the stop signs should be replaced with traffic lights. It uses strong, persuasive language, and asks the audience to take specific action within his/her abilities. Example 2 would probably receive the lowest score, a 1 or a 2, because it does not take a position or persuade the reader to take any specific action. While it does identify the problem, it does so in a somewhat confusing manner. The third example would fall in the middle of the rubric range. Although it takes a position, it could be clearer and more specific. It argues for the reader to take action, but the author could use stronger words for emphasis and make a specific request of the reader.

Comprehensiveness

The second skill examined through the Interdisciplinary Writing rubric is comprehensiveness. Can you read, and use, the information from all of the source material on the topic to support your position? The exam provides you with three articles to read that address the issue. The assessors will determine whether and how well you incorporate information from each of the articles to make and support your position.

To do well on this skill, you need to show that you can extract and incorporate information from the provided source material in order to formulate a clear argument supported by appropriate details. In other words, you need to be able to state your reasons for your position in your own words and be able to support those reasons with specific evidence from the provided sources. You do not need to quote or cite the sources, but, if you do quote, you *must* provide a citation. Also, it is a good idea to identify the title and/or author for specific data or details, even when you do not quote, so that the assessor has no doubt that you referenced the source. You do not need to refer to all three sources for each of the reasons you provide to support your position. However, you will show that you have developed this skill better if you use at least two of the sources for each reason.

If you take a look at the full rubric for the Interdisciplinary Writing in Chapter 1, you will note that the second item at each score point level addresses how comprehensive your writing is. The table below shows the criteria for this skill.

Figure 3.3: Score Criteria for Comprehensiveness

Score Point	Criteria
1	The response offers little or no support from the source materials, OR the support provided is copied verbatim.
2	The response contains only superficial support and/or may use information from only one or two of the source materials.
3	The response contains limited support and may not use information from each of the source materials.
4	The response contains adequate support but may not use information from each of the source materials.
5	The position is well supported, typically using information from each of the source materials.
6	The position is richly supported with information from each of the source materials.

Take a couple of minutes to read over the criteria at each level. Highlight the descriptive words that seem to be the key for determining how well you did at this skill. Jot down what it is that the assessors are looking for at each advanced level. In doing so, consider the following:

- How do the criteria for a score of 3 differ from the criteria for a score of 1 or 2?
- What is the biggest difference between the criteria for a score of 3 and the criteria for a score of 4?
- What do you need to do to raise your score from 4 to 5 or 6?

You probably noticed from the criteria that the assessors are truly looking for you to use all three sources to support your position. Incorporating information from each article will help you show that you can use your resources to make a stronger argument. Note that under the criteria for a score of 1 the assessors are looking for original wording. They do not want you to copy from the three sources word for word (which is what verbatim, used in the rubric, means). They want to see you take the information from the sources and put it together to make your own ideas about the problem. If you do not make the writing your own, and instead simply string together the words of the authors of the sources, you will not succeed on this test, even if you do use information from each source. If you gather data and examples from the three readings to develop strong reasons to support your position on the task, you will do very well.

Supporting Your Argument

The third skill the assessors look for in your writing is how well you support your argument. No matter what position you take, the assessors want to see that you can provide and support reasons for your position.

As discussed above, most of your support, in the form of details, examples, data, and quotes, will come from the three articles you are given to read. You may also use information from personal experience to give the work a sense of reality about your understanding of the problem. You will want to read the articles carefully to make sure that the evidence you use for your support does not contradict your position, and that it is relevant to what you are trying to explain. After you have added the supporting details from the source readings, you need to provide a clear explanation of how they validate your reason. This will make your argument stronger and clearer.

If you take a look at the full rubric for the Interdisciplinary Writing in Chapter 1, you will note that the third item at each score point level addresses how well you support your argument. Figure 3.4 below shows the criteria for this skill.

Score Point	Criteria
1	The support may be emotional, inaccurate, and irrelevant, or show serious misunderstanding.
2	The supporting ideas may be poorly developed and/or illogical and inconsistent; the information may be inaccurate or irrelevant.
3	The supporting ideas are few and/or only somewhat developed; some information may be inaccurate or irrelevant.
4	The supporting ideas are adequately but not thoroughly developed; some information may be inaccurate or irrelevant.
5	The supporting ideas are generally well developed; information is accurate and relevant.
6	The supporting ideas are very well developed; information is accurate and relevant.

If you take a close look at some of these criteria, you will see that they convey some very specific information about what the assessors will be examining. You probably noticed right away that the use of emotional support is not what they want to see. Some people think that persuasive writing demands an emotional tone. However, you should not confuse persuasiveness with emotional arguments. Persuasive writing *may* include some wording that triggers the emotions of the reader so that he or she is moved to take action, but it should mainly provide factual support to reinforce your position. Emotional writing, where the writer displays emotions through writing, is tricky, because it can distract the reader. Emotional writing can be characterized through the use of slang, too many superlatives (words that end in *–est* or otherwise express all or greatest extent), and a lack of factual details to back up the argument. Here is an example of emotional writing, using our intersection problem. As you read, underline the words in this example that make it emotional.

> You cannot vote to have a traffic light put into the Burke and Main intersection. It is a stupid idea and the whole thing is a waste of money. Whoever wanted this must be an overprotective and fearful person and doesn't have any common sense about how to use an intersection with stop signs, just like those people who get into accidents.

In this example, the writer makes judgments about the idea and the person(s) behind the idea which may or may not be accurate. However, the emotional nature of the writing has prevented the writer from providing supporting details to back up his argument. Even if the writer did provide some of those details, words such as "stupid," "waste," and "overprotective" tend to dominate the reader's attention, preventing the reader from focusing on the intended argument. Stick to the facts and data that support your arguments, and let them, instead of emotional appeals, trigger the emotions in your reader.

In addition to avoiding emotional language in your CAPT writing, you should also be sure to use accurate and relevant support from the source materials. Be sure that your data is correct and relates to your argument. You do not want to mislead or confuse the reader with information that is not relevant to your argument. For instance, if you are writing about the problem at the intersection of Burke and Main and are asking to have a traffic light installed, you probably do not want to mention unrelated ideas such as the number of potholes that were there two years ago. Stay focused on the topic and your argument will be stronger.

To build a strong argument, you need to understand the evidence you use. Be sure to avoid using any facts or data in the sources that you do not understand. If the information does not make sense to you, don't use it. There will be enough other information that you understand for you to use in your response. Similarly, you also want to make sure the details you choose from the sources as support for your argument logically connect to your reason. If you cannot do this, then your support may not be logical and that information should be removed.

You also want to ensure that your ideas are thoroughly developed. Do not assume that an idea speaks for itself. When making an argument, explain how the supporting evidence works together to explain the argument better. Take a look at the following examples that use support from the source materials.

Version 1

Another reason the intersection at Burke and Main needs traffic lights is because the pedestrian traffic has increased. There is that new store on Solomon Street, and there is a parking lot off Burke. According to the article by John Smith, the percentage of people using the lot has increased by ten percent since the store opened. According to the article by Mr. Jones, the store will be having sales every weekend. So, the light will help keep the pedestrians safe.

Version 2

Another reason the intersection at Burke and Main needs traffic lights is because the pedestrian traffic has increased. There is a new athletic apparel store on Solomon Street, and there is a parking lot off Burke. You only have to walk two blocks from the parking lot to the store, but you have to cross Main Street to get there. According to the article by John Smith, the percentage of people using the lot has increased by ten percent since the store opened, which indicates that there is a ten percent increase in the number of pedestrians crossing at the Burke and Main intersection. Steven Jones stated in his article that the store is going to start having sales every weekend, which could likely cause more pedestrian traffic between the parking lot on Burke and the new store. With an increase in pedestrian traffic, there is greater need to put in traffic and walk lights to help keep pedestrians safe.

What are the differences between version 1 and version 2? Before you read on, take a moment to jot them down.

The biggest difference is that the writer in version 2 explains how the supporting information relates to the problem. Take a look at Figure 3.5, which shows in italics the places the evidence is explained and connected to the reasoning for installing the traffic light at the intersection. Version 1, on the other hand, includes the support, but does not clearly show how it relates to the argument and reasoning. Version 2 does a better job because it connects the support to the arguments.

Selecting relevant evidence from your source materials is only one way to enhance your argument. The way you organize your thoughts also plays a great role in developing your thoughts.

Figure 3.5: Explaining the Evidence

> Another reason the intersection at Burke and Main needs traffic lights is because the pedestrian traffic has increased. There is that new athletic apparel store on Solomon Street, and there is a parking lot off Burke. You only have to walk two blocks from the parking lot to the store, *but you have to cross Main Street to get there.* According to the article by John Smith, the percentage of people using the lot has increased by ten percent since the store opened, *which indicates that there is a ten percent increase in the number of pedestrians crossing at the Burke and Main intersection.* Steven Jones stated in his article that the store is going to start having sales every weekend, *which could likely cause more pedestrian traffic between the parking lot on Burke and the new store. With an increase in pedestrian traffic, there is greater need to put in traffic and walk lights* to help keep pedestrians safe.

Organization

Organization is a requirement for good writing. The ideas must follow some sort of pattern that makes the writer's point clear and understandable. If you put your ideas in a random order, your readers will be confused and may disregard what you are trying to say. The reader might decide it is simply too much work to figure out your point or might just assume it will not make sense. The best way to produce successfully organized writing is to have a plan for your writing that focuses on a main idea and relates each subsequent point to that idea.

There are many ways to organize a piece of writing, some of which, depending on your purpose, are more effective than others. Generally, whether you are writing fiction, an essay, a poem, or a letter, you will introduce your topic and hint at the subtopics in the first few phrases or sentences of your work. Similarly, you will restate them at the end of the piece in a way that wraps up everything you said and ties it to your focus. What you do in the middle can progress in a variety of ways, again depending on your purpose, topic, and writing style.

There is no required format to organize your CAPT Interdisciplinary Writing response; however, Chapter 6 discusses one in particular that can be very helpful in helping you to stay focused. Refer to Figure 3.6 to begin to familiarize yourself with it at this time. Note how it provides you a guideline for the overall product, as well as for the individual paragraphs. Following this, or another outline, will help you to stick to your task of persuading someone to take a certain action.

Figure 3.6: Sample Organizational Format

I. Introduction
    A. Identify the issue
    B. State your position
    C. State your arguments
        1. Argument 1
        2. Argument 2
        3. Argument 3
    D. State the opposing side*
    E. Ask the reader to consider your position based on the arguments you make

II. Argument 1
    A. Restate the first argument you noted in your introduction. This should be your strongest argument.
    B. Explain what your argument means in your own words
    C. Provide your supporting evidence from at least two of your sources
        1. Be specific—details, facts, numbers
        2. Identify your sources; use quotes when necessary
        3. Explain in your own words how the evidence supports your argument
    D. State why the argument should convince the reader of your position

III. Argument 2
    A. Restate the second argument you noted in your introduction
    B. Explain what your argument means in your own words
    C. Provide your supporting evidence from at least two of your sources
        1. Be specific—details, facts, numbers
        2. Identify your sources; use quotes when necessary
        3. Explain in your own words how the evidence supports your argument
    D. State why the argument should convince the reader of your position.

IV. Argument 3
    A. Restate the third argument you noted in your introduction
    B. Explain what your argument means in your own words
    C. Provide your supporting evidence from at least two of your sources
        1. Be specific—details, facts, numbers
        2. Identify your sources; use quotes when necessary
        3. Explain in your own words how the evidence supports your argument
    D. State why the argument should convince the reader of your position

V. Opposing View*
    A. Recognize the other side has an opinion that may be logical
    B. State one of the reasons/evidence the other side may use
    C. Explain why that reason/evidence is not sufficient to choose that position
        1. Counter with evidence from your position
        2. Be respectful of the other side

VI. Conclusion
    A. State the issue again and why it is important to you that the reader agree with your position
    B. Restate the arguments briefly
    C. Thank the reader for his/her time and consideration

* Optional

If you take a look at the rubric for the Interdisciplinary Writing, you will note that the fourth item at each score point level addresses how well your writing is organized. The table below shows the criteria for this skill.

Figure 3.7: Score Criteria for Organization

Score Point	Criteria
1	The response lacks focus and a controlling idea; little or no organization is present, and frequent digressions and/or abrupt shifts in the response interfere with the meaning.
2	The response may lack focus and a controlling idea; digressions and/or abrupt shifts in the response interfere with the meaning.
3	The response is somewhat organized, but there may be digressions or abrupt shifts that interfere with the meaning.
4	The response is adequately organized with at least one controlling idea; digressions, if present, are not disruptive.
5	The response is well organized and contains one or more controlling ideas; digressions are rare.
6	The response is unified and focused and contains one or more controlling ideas; organization and control are sustained throughout the response.

The criteria for this skill are pretty straightforward. If your writing is focused on your central idea and you stick to the argument you are making, you will do fine on this aspect. You want to make sure that the support you give through reasons and examples are directly related to your point and that you do not bring in other details that are unrelated. While unrelated information may be interesting, it will cause confusion in your writing. Here is an example of a piece of writing with digressions, or unrelated information, that cause disruptions that interfere with meaning:

Example

Traffic lights will make it safer for pedestrians who cross the road at the intersection of Burke and Main. The tall blue mailbox is on the southwest corner of that intersection. Sometimes people run across the street between cars and do not wait for it to be safe. Nancy Oliver noted in her article that three people this year alone have been hospitalized because they were hit at this intersection. With the increase in pedestrian traffic due to the new store's location in relation to the parking lot on Burke (see John Smith's article) this number could rise. The parking lot on Burke is a lot nicer than it used to be with all the new flowers and trees. With a streetlight to tell people when it is safe to cross, people walking will be safer at this intersection.

While it may be that there is a mailbox at the intersection, this sentence is unrelated to the rest of the paragraph. Including it here distracts the reader from the point the writer is trying to make, and causes the writing to be harder to understand. Similarly, while it may be interesting that the parking lot is nicer, it has very little, if anything, to do with the safety of pedestrians. Leave out the unrelated information so that the reader can focus directly on your point, understand your view, and be persuaded by your argument.

If you have a plan or format for your writing, you will also show that you have developed the last skill that is assessed on this test: Clarity and Fluency. Your writing will be much more polished if it is organized; this organization allows your words to flow.

Clarity and Fluency

The last skill that the assessors examine in your writing is how well you choose your words and put them together. *Clarity* means how clear you make your writing; *fluency* is how smoothly your writing flows. These together give your paper a voice. Clear and fluent writing conveys your meaning without jolting or confusing your reader by your word choices, sentence structure, or transitions. The goal is to have your reader think about your focus instead of the individual words you choose or how you put them together.

Your writing is most clear when you choose and organize your words appropriately. You need to think about meaning, audience, and emphasis. The more specific words you can choose (e.g., pedestrian instead of person, fatalities instead of accidents), the better—unless it is a word that it is too difficult or technical for your reader. Be wary of using decorative or complex words, however. You do not want the reader to have to stop reading to figure out what a word means. For example, while you may think that streetlights "obstruct the mountainous scenery," you would probably explain to a young child that the "streetlights get in the way of seeing the mountains." The words "mountainous scenery" might confuse and distract a young reader.

As for fluency, you should try to write so that your ideas flow. Your sentence structure should be varied. Too many short sentences will cause the reader to be distracted by the short rhythm. Too many long sentences may confuse your reader. Also, your transitions should be smooth, taking the reader from what you are talking about into what you will be discussing next. For instance, this discussion on clarity and fluency is going to move into a discussion of the criteria for assessing these skills.

If you take a look at the rubric for the Interdisciplinary Writing in Chapter 1, you will note that the fifth item at each score point level addresses the clarity and fluency of your writing. The table below shows the criteria for this skill.

Figure 3.8: Score Criteria for Clarity and Fluency

Score Point	Criteria
1	Many ideas are difficult to understand; fluency and transitions are lacking.
2	Some ideas may be difficult to understand; fluency and transitions are lacking.
3	Some ideas may not be clearly expressed; fluency and transitions may be lacking.
4	Most ideas are clear and understandable, but fluency and transitions may be lacking.
5	Most ideas are clearly expressed; writing is generally fluent, with some use of transitions.
6	The ideas are clearly and effectively developed; writing is fluent and polished with effective transitions.

These criteria are pretty straightforward. You want to make sure that your readers understand your writing. The best way to achieve this is to practice writing and reading your work aloud to yourself. You will recognize the rhythm created by your word choice, sentence structure, and transitions by noticing where you stumble as you read. If you stumble over the words, choose different phrasing or find an appropriate synonym for one of the words. When you cannot make sense of what you hear yourself say, go back and rework that sentence or paragraph. If you run out of breath before you finish reading a sentence, it could be a run-on or simply too wordy, and should be shortened or divided into more than one sentence. If your thoughts seem to leap from one idea to another, check your transitions between sentences and paragraphs.

You have been working on these skills since you first started writing sentences, and they should be recognizable to you at this point. If you find that you have a weakness in this area and practicing does not seem to help, you might want to ask a teacher you work with well for extra help, or refer to one of the writing process books referred to in the Appendix.

Skills Summary

You have been working on developing and refining all of the skills assessed by the Interdisciplinary Writing task over the last several years. None of this should be new to you, nor should it scare you. You use these skills in most of your classes, and you will continue to use them long after the CAPT is a distant memory to you. The point of this book is not to teach you something new; rather it is to give you an overview and short review of what is expected of you on the writing portion of the CAPT. Take the information that is helpful to you and use it to improve your writing, and, as a result, your test score.

Also, remember that the writing that is being assessed is a first draft of a persuasive letter. The assessors know that your time to produce the piece is limited, and while they look for certain evidence of the skills, they will not give you a lower score because of a slip or two. The few people who earn a 6 are writers by nature and really do not struggle with the process or using words. However, most test-takers will be in the 3–5 range on the rubric.

Now that you know the specific skills the assessors examine, it is time to take a look at the actual test and what it asks you to do.

Chapter 4:
Interdisciplinary Writing Test–The Task

As noted earlier, the Interdisciplinary Writing test requires you to complete a writing assignment. You are given three articles to read about a specific issue that you must use as the basis for writing a persuasive letter to a specified person arguing that he or she take a particular action. Understanding the assignment is your first step to succeeding on this test. Each test booklet contains a set of instructions that will help you understand your task.

Test Instructions

You may be surprised to find two pages of instructions on the writing test. Two pages of instructions may seem like a lot to read; however, the instructions provide you with the information that you will need to complete the assignment successfully. The instructions explain the issue you will be addressing, tell you what it is you are trying to persuade your audience to do, and direct you to address the letter to a particular audience. Following is a breakdown of the CAPT Interdisciplinary Writing instruction pages.

- **Overview**—The overview explains that you are writing a persuasive letter based on three articles on a certain issue. It also notes that you will be required to take a position on the issue and support that position using each of the source articles provided with the test. The overview does not contain any information that should be new to you if you have had any practice on this test or if you have worked through this book.
- **About This Test**—This section of the instructions identifies the problem that you will be reading about in the articles. It also reminds you that you should use the skills and knowledge you have developed through your learning in all educational disciplines.

- **The Issue**—This part of the instructions is extremely important to read and understand because it clearly sets forth the issue and the problem for you. It will introduce you to the topic of the articles and summarize the two sides of the issue. You will choose one of the viewpoints noted in "The Issue" to argue in your persuasive writing.

- **Your Task**—Here you will find out what you need to do and who your audience is. The task is usually to write a persuasive letter or editorial. The audience is usually a newspaper editor, a political representative, or someone who can take action to address the problem. This paragraph will also clearly describe how you should present the position you take. Generally, you can rephrase the sentence from that paragraph to use in your first paragraph to ensure that you clearly ask your audience to take the action you want. For instance, the "Your Task" section may state:

  > In your letter you must persuade your city council person to
  > support or oppose the change from stop signs to traffic lights at
  > the intersection of Burke and Main streets.

  If you choose to *support* the change in your writing, you would then include a sentence such as the following:

  > I strongly urge you to support the use of traffic lights instead of stop
  > signs at the Burke and Main intersection.

  Do not be afraid to use the same words as those given to you in the "Your Task" paragraph. Doing so will ensure that you clearly present your position to your reader, as well as help you stay focused on the issue throughout the writing.

  The "Your Task" part of the instructions also summarizes the process and order for completing the task. It advises you to read each of the articles on the issue before taking a position, choose a position and support it with evidence from the source materials, plan before you write, and then write your answer in the booklet provided. You are reminded here what your topic is: to include information from each source and your personal experience (if you wish), and finally, that you have only three pages on which to submit your response.

- **Your Score**—This section tells you what skills will be assessed and how. The test includes a copy of the rubric, which you can refer to during the test period if necessary. This part of the instructions also reminds you to "Read, Think, Plan, and Write," as is suggested under the "Your Task" section.

While the instructions for each Interdisciplinary Writing task are generally the same from test to test (except for the issue and what you must specifically do), it is a good idea to reread them before you begin each test. This will help you to refresh your memory so that you do not make any mistakes in following directions which could result in a lower score.

Reading the Articles

You may wonder whether you *really* need to read all the articles. The short answer to that question is: YES, you really do need to read each of the articles. Once you have read the instructions and are clear on what the assignment and the issue are, you need to start reading the articles efficiently and critically. As discussed in Chapter 3, part of your score is based on whether and to what extent you refer to each of the source materials provided with the test. Not referencing each of the articles will keep you from achieving a score of a 5 or 6. Therefore, in order to accurately and appropriately reference the source materials, you need to read them. Here are some hints to help you read effectively with your purpose in mind.

Time Savers

You want to read as quickly as you can while still understanding the meaning of the articles. You have 55 minutes to complete the reading, choose your position, plan your writing, and prepare your draft. You need to use this time wisely. Here are some ways to save time while you read.

1. **Remember your purpose and your task.** At the top of your scrap paper, copy the sentence from the "Your Task" section which tells you the issue you are to consider. Refer to it repeatedly as you read so that you do not get sidetracked by other issues that might be discussed in the materials.
2. **Review the title, publisher, and section headings for hints about topics and bias.** Sometimes you can tell from this information what side the author might be more inclined to support, and that can give you a clue about what information you might find in that article or section.
3. **Look for and highlight key words and phrases that indicate the pros and the cons of the issue.** Words such as *should, must, never, always, problematic, cure, cause,* and *result* can help you find important information supporting one side or the other. Bring two different colored highlighters to the test: use one to highlight information that supports the pro side and the other to highlight the ideas that support the con side.
4. **Look for and highlight key facts, including *numbers* and *percentages,* which support pros and cons.** The numbers will help you to support your position as you write your letter, and highlighting them in the article will make them stand out so that you can find them easily to record them accurately in your writing.

There are also some problems you should *avoid* while reading. Understanding them will help you to use your time effectively.

1. **Vocabulary frustration**—Try not to get bogged down in vocabulary that you do not know. Try one or two skills, such as reading in context or breaking the word into smaller words to help you get the meaning. If these do not work, underline the word and go back to it if you have time and it is necessary for you to understand the material. Remember, if you do not understand part of the source, *do not* use that piece in your own writing to support your position. Doing so could adversely affect your response.

2. **Technical words and phrases**—If you come across words and phrases that are highly technical or confusing, skip them. The time you use to figure them out could be used to write your paper more fluently and clearly. You should be able to find enough other information to support your argument without including them.

3. **Emotional reactions**—Remember that getting too emotional about the issue can prevent you from developing a sound and *rational* argument. You want to focus on taking a stand and defending it logically. Therefore, when you read, look for supporting evidence, including facts and data; do not focus on the emotional aspect of the problem.

There are many other ways you can improve your reading, many of which you have probably learned throughout your education. For example, you can read all the section headings, or the introduction and conclusion, before reading the full text so that you have an idea of the author's goals. Make sure you use those skills that you already know work for you, and try out any of the above ideas that may be new to you.

Taking Notes

Taking notes while you read can help you retain information and recall it more quickly. You should highlight key words and phrases, and indicate whether they support the pro or con position of the issue. As noted above, you might want to use two different highlighters to differentiate between two sides of the argument. This will make sorting the information and finding appropriate examples and details easier as you are planning and writing.

You can also jot down notes on the articles themselves, indicating where you find the ideas or points most interesting. Use the margins to note connections with your prior experience, or indicate that a similar point was made in another article. You can also write down the reasons given to support the position as well as specific examples that support those reasons.

No matter what techniques you use to read more efficiently and productively, you need to make sure that you are reading each of the articles with *purpose*. Becoming a good writer starts with being a good reader. The time you put into developing your reading skills will help you develop your writing skills as well.

Using the Charts Provided

The test packet comes with two charts for you to use in the note-taking and planning stages of your writing. One chart should be used to record arguments and evidence supporting the issue, and the other to record information about the opposing position. You are not required to use the charts to help you take this test, but if you do use them, you may find it easier to choose a position to defend and to organize your writing.

The charts are very simple to use: In one column you record your argument; in the other you record your evidence. You should also note on the chart where you obtained the information about each argument and supporting evidence. If you think you will want to quote any phrases or data from the articles, you should use quotation marks on the chart to help you to remember to do so in your response. Having this information on the chart will make it readily available as you write and you will save time by not having to search for it in the articles.

In the first column of your chart, you should record your arguments for taking the position: either for or against. For instance, one argument to have traffic lights installed would be to provide a safer path for pedestrians. You record the evidence and support for the arguments in the other column. Your evidence is the information from the source materials that supports your argument. For instance, support for traffic lights providing a safer path for pedestrians could include data on the number of pedestrian accidents at the intersection in the recent past, or the percentage decrease in pedestrian accidents at other intersections with similar traffic volume that have traffic lights.

There are usually three to four arguments to support a position in the type of writing you are doing. Similarly, you will be provided with 3–4 pieces of evidence or data to support each argument in the articles. Your position is the broadest statement, the arguments get a bit more specific, and the evidence is the most specific. Here is a visual to help you remember:

Figure 4.1: Supporting Your Position

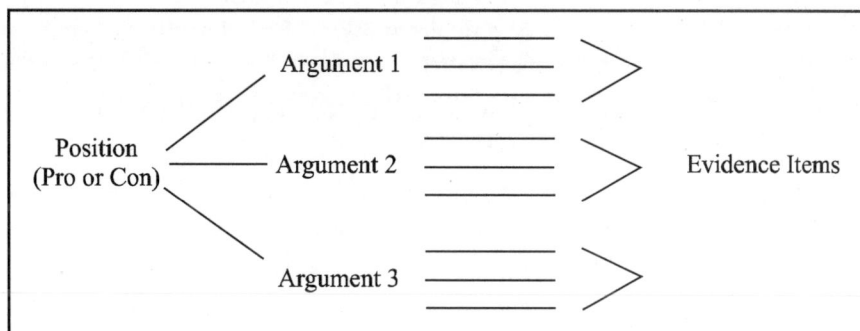

Figure 4.2 provides an example of a chart much like the one provided on the CAPT. The arguments and supporting evidence are recorded on it. You will note that there is evidence from two or all three sources supporting each argument. While you may record all the data as you conduct your initial reading, you may decide to go back for additional information after you are done. For instance, you may have only two pieces of evidence to support an argument

that you know you can strengthen. You might go back to the articles to find some more information. Or, you may want to get more evidence from one of the articles to ensure that you have been comprehensive in your response.

Sometimes, as you are reading, you may not be able to state your argument clearly. In those instances, jot down ideas about what the argument is—i.e., safety—and fill it in with a more complete thought later.

Figure 4.2 Sample Note-Taking Chart

Arguments *supporting* the change from stop signs to traffic lights at the intersection of Burke and Main	Supporting Evidence or Claims
The number and severity of accidents at the intersection have increased recently.	• 4 accidents in the last month (Jones) • 3 accidents resulted in hospitalizations in the past 4 months (Smith) • Oliver states "20% of all traffic injuries in our city that are reported to the 5 largest insurance companies occur at the intersection of Burke and Main."
People do not drive safely at that intersection.	• Smith counted 25 people in a four-hour period that did not come to a complete stop at the stop sign. • 40 percent of drivers making a turn at the intersection failed to use their turn signal (Smith). • People are confused about right of way laws and become aggressive when waiting for their turn (Oliver).
There has been an increase in pedestrian traffic.	• New store on Solomon Street means more people are walking from parking lot on Burke across Main (Jones). • New store increasing special sales on the weekends (Jones). • Parking lot on Burke has seen a 10% increase in use since new store opened (Smith). • Smith's visual study of the intersection showed that 72 people crossed Main Street at Burke in a four-hour period, "a 70% increase over the number of people who walked through that intersection at the time the stop signs were installed 28 years ago."

Once you have the charts completed, you can use them to help you think about the issue and choose a position. Whether you agree with one view or the other may not be as important as whether you have collected enough evidence to write a persuasive argument. While believing in your position could assist you in your persuasiveness, a lack of supporting evidence could prevent you from doing well. Therefore, examine your charts and determine which position has *the strongest argument and the best evidence* for you to use. A thorough defense will be more persuasive with the more specific support you can provide. If your pro and con evidence is equal, choose the position you most agree with.

Sometimes students cannot decide which side to take. If you see valid points for both sides, you may want to always take the pro position, unless the source material provides you with a stronger argument in your opinion. That way, you won't spend so much time trying to decide what position to take. Remember, you must pick one side or the other.

Once you have decided on a position, you are ready to write. You have already done most of the work, if you used the charts, by organizing your arguments and evidence. Now you have to tie it all together by explaining in an organized, persuasive manner how the arguments support your position and how the evidence supports your argument.

Chapter 5:
Interdisciplinary Writing Test–Completing the Task

As you write your response, you will want to keep in mind the rubric and the skills that are being assessed. Chapter 3 focused on the rubric in detail, but now you need to understand it in light of the actual task. A copy of the rubric is provided again at the end of this chapter for your convenience, but remember to refer back to Chapter 3 for more specific discussion of the rubric criteria for each score point level. The skills, as they relate to the task, are discussed below in the same order that they were in Chapter 3.

Your task on this test is to take a pro or con position on a particular issue and persuasively argue that position to a specified audience.

Taking a Clear Position

Your introductory paragraph will generally determine how well you show your skills for taking a clear and persuasive position. You want to keep your introduction fairly simple and succinct (to the point), firmly stating your position and reasons, while keeping the details to explain in the body of the letter. The reader will have no doubt about your understanding of the issue or your position if you start your response by restating the problem given to you in the instructions, and then stating whether you agree or disagree with the decision or proposed resolution. (For help on choosing a position, refer to the section on using the charts at the end of Chapter 4.)

Keep It Simple

The problem is stated for you very clearly at least three times in the instructions. Use the language the instructions give you, restating it only to the extent that makes it work for your assigned writing purpose. For example, if you are beginning a response on the issue about traffic lights, the example given throughout this book, you might write the following:

> Dear City Council Person:
> I understand that you are considering replacing the stop signs at the intersection of Burke and Main with traffic lights. I believe that you should vote yes on this issue.

Note the simplicity of the introductory sentences. They provide a minimal summary of the issue and state the writer's position on the proposed action. The key is to state the issue and then your position—without adding any extra thoughts or reasons. Doing this serves two purposes: clarifying that you know what the issue is and advising your reader what the letter is addressing.

Once you have stated the issue and your position, you want to briefly mention your reasons for taking that position. Whether you used the charts provided with the test or not, you should have an idea of what the arguments and supporting evidence are. Choose the three strongest arguments, and state them briefly after you have identified your position. Do not include any of your supporting evidence in the introduction. The reasons will become the focus of each of your body paragraphs and you will provide your support there. Again using the traffic light example, the third sentence of your letter may appear as follows:

> The traffic lights are necessary because people do not drive safely at that intersection with only stop signs there, the number and severity of accidents has risen significantly recently, and there is an increase in the amount of pedestrian traffic.

Note that supporting evidence is not used in the introduction. At this stage you simply need to provide an overview of the issue, your position, and your arguments. Make these words your mantra (words you repeat to help you focus) to help you remember how you can start off on the right foot:

ISSUE → POSITION → ARGUMENTS

As you write the rest of your letter, the introductory paragraph will guide you. Hints on how to complete the letter in such a way that you maintain what you began in the introduction is discussed in the upcoming section on organization.

Address Your Audience

The last thing you need to remember about taking a position is to be aware of your audience. You should consider the following types of questions:

- What does the reader already know about the topic?
- What do you want to make sure the reader knows about your reasons?
- What can the reader do about the problem?

- How can I convince the reader to take the action I want?
- What tone should I use with this reader?

Your goal is to provide enough information to show the reader that you understand the issue, but not so much that you insult your reader's knowledge. You also do not want to present complicated, technical information that will serve to confuse your reader. If your council person does not have a background in engineering, you probably do not want to discuss the complications of installing traffic lights in any great detail. You should be respectful as well as conscientious of what action your audience can actually take or not take. Do not ask the council person to remove the stop signs herself; that is not her job. Also, be sure to *ask,* and not order or threaten, your reader to take the action you want. Remember, throughout your writing, that you want the reader to agree with you. To gain the reader's support, your tone must be respectful and appropriate.

The first sentences you write should clearly show your awareness of audience. Your introduction sets the tone for the rest of the assignment, and following the plan (issue, position, arguments) you will be off to a great start. Developing your position through the remainder of the letter will be much easier if you begin simply, clearly, and respectfully. Figure 5.1 shows the sample introduction as a whole, with the different parts identified.

Figure 5.1: Sample Introduction

	Dear City Council Person:
State the issue:	I understand that you are considering replacing the stop signs at the intersection of Burke and Main with traffic
State your position:	lights. I believe that you should vote yes on this issue. The
State your arguments:	traffic lights are necessary because people do not drive safely at that intersection with only stop signs there, the number and severity of accidents have risen significantly recently, and there is an increase in the amount of pedestrian
State your goal:	traffic. I hope that after you have read my reasoning below, you agree with my position.

Proving Your Writing Is Comprehensive

Before we discuss how to continue on the solid path you have started with your introduction, you want to be sure that as you write the body of your letter you are meeting the criteria for *comprehensiveness.* Make sure you are supporting your position with evidence and data from each of the source materials provided. Try to keep your evidence balanced by referring to at least two of the sources for each argument. To make your support rich and meaningful, try to use two pieces of relevant evidence from each source in your essay. You may not always be able to do so, but aiming for that end will help you to meet the higher criteria standards.

Developing Your Supporting Ideas

As you write the body paragraphs, you want to consider how you will maintain your persuasiveness. The way to do that is to make sure you provide sufficient support for your arguments. For each argument, which will each have its own body paragraph, you want to use appropriate support from the source materials. Back up the arguments with evidence that is logical and factual, rather than emotional. As discussed in Chapter 3, an emotional argument may have the opposite effect on your reader than you intend.

Make sure that your information is *accurate*. If you use information from an article that is recorded in your writing inaccurately, you will not only lose credibility but you could accidentally change the meaning of your support and weaken your argument as well. Accurate information will help maintain the logical connections between your arguments and the supporting evidence you provide.

You also need to choose *relevant* supporting evidence for your arguments. If you are discussing the idea that there has been a recent increase in accidents at Burke and Main, you should avoid discussing the severity of an accident that occurred 15 years ago. While it may be interesting, it detracts from your argument and distracts the reader. Remember that your focus is on the *increase* in accidents, not their severity.

As you write your supporting evidence into your response, you need to connect it to the argument. If you cannot write a sentence to connect the examples to the argument, your evidence is likely not relevant to your argument and should be left out.

Connecting your evidence is another good way to ensure that you are developing your support. Find evidence from one article that supports evidence from another and then tie them together with your own thoughts. This will enhance not only in meeting the criteria for developing your supporting ideas, but also show a higher skill level in persuasiveness and comprehensiveness. Figure 5.2 is a good example of a body paragraph that connects supporting ideas.

Figure 5.2: Sample Body Paragraph

Evidence from Source 1: Evidence from Source 2:	Another reason the intersection at Burke and Main needs traffic lights is because the pedestrian traffic has increased. There is that new athletic apparel store on Solomon Street, and there is a parking lot off Burke. You have to walk only two blocks from the parking lot to the store, but you have to cross Main Street to get there. According to the article by John Smith, the percentage of people using the lot has increased by ten percent since the store opened, which indicates that there is a ten percent increase in the number of pedestrians crossing at the Burke and Main intersection. Steven Jones stated in his article that the store is going to start having sales every weekend, which could likely cause more pedestrian traffic between the parking lot on Burke and the new store. With an increase in pedestrian traffic, there is greater need to put in traffic and walk lights to help keep pedestrians safe.

Note that in this example the writer used and connected supporting evidence from Smith and Jones: the increased use of the parking lot across Main since the store opened and new sales on the weekends that could lead to an even larger increase in pedestrian traffic. By combining the ideas, you will develop your supporting ideas more thoroughly and originally and, therefore, increase your persuasiveness and effectiveness.

Having a plan for your writing will increase your ability to provide adequate support. The plan ensures that you add details that are necessary to back up your reasoning.

Organization

If there is one skill element assessed on the Interdisciplinary Writing test that all the other elements depend upon, it is how well you organize your writing. If you do not have a plan and you insert ideas in no apparent order, you will confuse your reader. If you lose the reader, then you have failed to develop a persuasive position, have made it extremely difficult to determine whether you have used your sources comprehensively, and given no way to determine whether you have accurately developed your supporting ideas with relevant evidence. You will also lose fluency and clarity, and you will definitely lack transitions. The organizational plan of your writing is the glue that holds everything else together.

There are various ways to organize your writing, some of which will work well with the format given on this test. You can use any format that works for you to complete this task, but the one introduced to you in Chapter 3 can help you make sure you are proving your skills. Before reading on, take a few minutes to review the sample organizational format in Figure 5.3.

Figure 5.3: Sample Organizational Format

I. Introduction
  A. Identify the issue
  B. State your position
  C. State your arguments
    1. Argument 1
    2. Argument 2
    3. Argument 3
  D. State the opposing side*
  E. Ask the reader to consider your position based on the arguments you make

II. Argument 1
  A. Restate the first argument you noted in your introduction. This should be your strongest argument.
  B. Explain what your argument means in your own words
  C. Provide your supporting evidence from at least two of your sources
    1. Be specific—details, facts, numbers
    2. Identify your sources; use quotes when necessary
    3. Explain in your own words how the evidence supports your argument
  D. State why the argument should convince the reader of your position

III. Argument 2
  A. Restate the second argument you noted in your introduction
  B. Explain what your argument means in your own words
  C. Provide your supporting evidence from at least two of your sources
    1. Be specific—details, facts, numbers
    2. Identify your sources; use quotes when necessary
    3. Explain in your own words how the evidence supports your argument
  D. State why the argument should convince the reader of your position.

IV. Argument 3
  A. Restate the third argument you noted in your introduction
  B. Explain what your argument means in your own words
  C. Provide your supporting evidence from at least two of your sources
    1. Be specific—details, facts, numbers
    2. Identify your sources; use quotes when necessary
    3. Explain in your own words how the evidence supports your argument
  D. State why the argument should convince the reader of your position

V. Opposing View*
  A. Recognize the other side has an opinion that may be logical
  B. State one of the reasons/evidence the other side may use
  C. Explain why that reason/evidence is not sufficient to choose that position
    1. Counter with evidence from your position
    2. Be respectful of the other side

VI. Conclusion
  A. State the issue again and why it is important to you that the reader agree with your position
  B. Restate the arguments briefly
  C. Thank the reader for his/her time and consideration

* Optional

Introduction

You probably noted that paragraph one, your introduction, is set out just as we discussed previously in the chapter. You start with identifying the issue, stating your position, and briefly mentioning your reasons, or arguments. Remember the mantra:

ISSUE → POSITION → ARGUMENTS

Arguments

Put your arguments in the order that you will present them in the body of the letter. This will add consistency and cohesiveness to the overall document, and strengthen it. You *may* choose to follow your reasons with an acknowledgment that some people disagree with your position, but if you do so, you must also indicate that you will show why your position is stronger. For example:

> Some people believe that the stop signs provide sufficient protection
> at this intersection. However, the evidence shows otherwise.

If you choose to do this, your fourth body paragraph (fifth paragraph of the letter) will then be a discussion of the alternative position and why it is not sufficient to change your, or your reader's, mind. You will also need to adjust your introductory paragraph so that it includes a sentence to acknowledge your audience's role and respectfully ask that the reader take the action you request.

Your second paragraph will begin with a restatement of your first, and strongest, argument, which should be the first one presented in your introductory paragraph. Tell the reader why this argument supports your position in your own words and then follow up with your evidence and data from your reading. Be sure to include support from at least two sources, and, where you can, provide two pieces of evidence from each source. Make sure you explain how the evidence supports your argument. Even if you think the connection is obvious, your persuasiveness and development will be stronger when you use your own words to tie it all together. Summarize the paragraph by restating how the argument you made supports your position. In other words, always connect your evidence back to your position.

Review the chart below in Figure 5.4, and then re-read the introduction example in Figure 5.1. Then, create a second paragraph, your first body paragraph, to insert in our streetlight example. Your paragraph should include all of the components listed in the chart, using specific details. You can refer to the completed chart from Figure 4.2 to help you with sample "evidence."

Figure 5.4: Organizing Your Arguments

Paragraph 2: Argument 1

    A. Restate the first argument you noted in your introduction. This should be your strongest argument

    B. Explain what your argument means in your own words

    C. Provide your supporting evidence from at least two of your sources

        1. Be specific—details, facts, numbers

        2. Identify your sources; use quotes when necessary

        3. Explain in your own words how the evidence supports your argument

    D. State why the argument should convince the reader of your position

Your third and fourth paragraphs will be similar to your second paragraph, except that they will address the second and third arguments and their supporting evidence. If you have completed the chart provided with the test, either while or after you read the source materials, this information should be easy to transfer into your draft response. The hardest part will be making logical connections and putting the ideas into your own words.

Addressing the Opposing Viewpoint

Your fifth body paragraph, if you choose to include it, will be your acknowledgment of the other side of the issue. Letting the reader know that you realize that people who take the other position might have strong arguments too will show that you have fully considered the issue and will make your writing more persuasive. However, you need to be sure to explain why their argument(s) are less convincing than yours. For example:

> Some people believe that the stops signs are sufficient protection for the Burke and Main intersection. They argue that more police presence at the intersection will reduce the amount of carelessness and accidents (Smith). However, they are not taking into consideration the increased number and severity of the accidents as well as the increase in the use of the intersection by pedestrians, whose safety will be better protected by crosswalks governed by streetlights. Putting in streetlights is the best, appropriate option.

In this example, the author states the position of the other side, but does not make an emotional attack. Rather, the writer points out that the other argument neglects to consider some of the information, making the opposing position questionable. This adds to the effectiveness of your argument and increases the persuasiveness of the writing overall.

Conclusion

You need to end the writing with a conclusion to wrap up your ideas. If you are running short of time, try to write at least one or two sentences at the end where you sum up your position and repeat your request. Be sure to acknowledge to the reader that you know his or her time is valuable and that you appreciate the time they took to read your letter and consider your position.

More Organization Tips

There are a couple of things you need to keep in mind as you write to keep you from straying from your writing plan. The main goal is to stay focused on your position and support it with relevant arguments and evidence. Throughout the paper, maintain a clear and decisive position, repeating it as often as you can, without overdoing it, to reaffirm your stance.

Within your paragraphs, be attentive to the specific argument you are making. Keep your ideas and the supporting evidence targeted toward that argument. Refer back to your first sentence of the paragraph as you think and write to help keep you focused. If you find that you are straying, correct your mistake as early as possible. Sometimes it is better to neatly cross out some words rather than trying to refocus by adding more words.

Clarity and Fluency

If organization is the glue that holds your work together in your writing, the way you craft your words is the glitter that makes it shine. Just as dressing up your artwork makes it more pleasing to the eye, giving your writing clarity and fluency makes it more pleasing to the reader's mind.

The more clearly you express yourself, the easier it will be for your reader to understand and follow your point. Clarity keeps the reader from halting periodically to try to figure out what you are saying. One way to improve your clarity is to keep your thoughts simple. This is especially important on the CAPT Interdisciplinary Writing test because you will likely be arguing a position about a topic that you may have just been exposed to within the last twenty minutes. You do not need to impress the reader with complex sentence structure or obscure vocabulary. Select words you know well so that you use them properly, as well as words your reader should know so that he or she can read without stopping to figure them out. Also, make sure that you avoid examples and evidence that you do not understand. If something does not make sense to you, you will probably not be able to explain it very well in your writing. If you have time while and after you write, you should reread your work and try to simplify any phrasing or vocabulary that may not be as clear as you planned.

Your writing will also be improved if you capture the natural rhythm of the English language. Keep your sentences varied—their length, structure, and emphasis will all play a role in the way the words flow when they are read. Using too many short sentences will make your reading choppy. Using too many long ones will cause your reader to stumble, or read too fast. If you start all your sentences the same way, or use the same structure such as subject-verb-object, the reader might lose interest. Mix up your patterns by using different styles of phrases for impact. For instance, if you want to emphasize a thought, work it into a short, simple sentence. To provide details, explanations, or comparisons, use longer sentences that start with a descriptive phrase instead of the subject. Most important, try to keep your sentences connected with a natural thought progression. The more fluent your writing, the easier to read, with more probability that your reader will not only finish it, but also think about it more seriously.

The Importance of These Skills

The CAPT Interdisciplinary Writing task is set up very specifically to assess the skills discussed in this chapter and throughout this text. While you may be an excellent creative or narrative writer, you will need to focus your writing on persuasive tactics for this test. Repeatedly reviewing the skills assessed, along with the rubric criteria before you take the tests, will help you to focus on them as you take the test.

Chapter 6:
Interdisciplinary Writing Test–Suggestions and Tips

In addition to practicing the skills that are assessed on the Interdisciplinary Writing test, you can ensure a higher score if you remember a few other tips. Issues such as time management, writing mechanics, following directions, and originality can all play a role in how well you perform.

This is a timed test: You have 55 minutes to read and analyze three articles on a specific issue, an issue about which you may not have any prior knowledge. You also have to plan what you will write and then write a full response, with an introduction, body, and conclusion that effectively argues your position. When you start reading, note the time and the halfway point of the testing period. If you find that you are reading beyond the halfway point, you need to stop yourself and skim the remaining article(s). If you find yourself working more slowly than you can afford, choose a position before you finish reading and look specifically for only that information that will help you to support that position.

As repeated throughout this book, you will be writing a first draft of a letter to a specific audience. Although handwriting, grammar, and spelling are not assessed, you should do your absolute best on these details while you write your response. If the assessors cannot read your work, or cannot make sense of it because of too many of these sorts of errors, it will be very difficult for them to determine your skill levels as compared to the rubric. The neater, more accurate work you do, the more successful you will be.

In addition to making your work as easy as possible to read, you need to make sure that you stick to the topic to avoid confusing the reader with unrelated information. Remember our mantra:

ISSUE → POSITION → ARGUMENTS

This will help you stay focused on the task of taking and arguing a position on the assigned issue. You also need to remember to keep all your paragraphs on evidence for the specific argument in the body of your letter. You should be able to avoid digression into an unrelated topic.

Even though the topic is assigned and you have to take one of two positions on the issue, you need to use your own words and original ideas. Copying or paraphrasing the articles too much will keep you from scoring well. The assessors want to see that you can take the ideas of others and put them together to create or develop your own ideas. Take what they give you and make it your own. Show them that you have put some thought into the matter, and are not merely restating what you read. If you remember to explain your examples and tie them to your arguments, you will not have a problem with this strategy.

While the last four chapters of this text may make you feel overwhelmed about the Interdisciplinary Writing task, you need to keep reminding yourself that you have learned the skills necessary to succeed on CAPT. You might need some practice, you might need some guidance and reminders, but you already know what you need to do.

Chapter 7: Revising Your Writing

Chapter 2 discussed the idea that writing is a process that includes several steps to get from idea to finished product. The Interdisciplinary Writing tasks examine your skills in the early stages of that process—brainstorming, planning, and drafting. The second part of the Writing Across the Disciplines test, Editing and Revising, examines your skills in being able to polish your writing before putting it into a final, polished format.

The focus of the editing and revising stages is on improving a piece of writing. Very few people can write a nearly perfect piece on a first attempt. Often it takes several revisions to get it as close to perfect as it can be. If you have ever worked with wood, think of what you do once you have completed putting your project together. You finish it by sanding off any rough edges, polishing metal components, and maybe adding a coat or two of varnish or paint. In writing, you revise in order to refine your work by:

- reorganizing it to improve your clarity
- restructuring sentences to increase the flow
- removing any unrelated or distracting material
- revisiting your vocabulary to determine whether you have chosen appropriate and precise terms to express your ideas

You also edit your work to ensure that you have used proper English by correcting errors in mechanics, grammar, punctuation, and spelling. In this way, you sand and polish your writing so that the reader is not distracted by the rough edges left by improper use of the language.

The Editing and Revising test consists of three written passages that are generally less than one page in length. These passages contain certain errors that you must fix by choosing the correct answers to eighteen multiple-choice questions. *The Connecticut Academic*

Performance Test Second Generation Reading and Writing Across the Disciplines Handbook lists the following areas that are assessed on this test:

- Composition (Revising)
  - Content, Organization, and Tone
  - Sentence Construction
  - Word Choice

- Editing
  - Capitalization
  - Punctuation
  - Usage
  - Spelling

This chapter will give you an overview of revising your writing. You will learn more about editing in Chapter 8. Remember, the information provided is intended to refresh your memory; it is not intended to be a sole source for your education on these skills. If you need additional help with any of the topics discussed below, please ask one of your teachers or your parents for specific help. There are also a variety of books that focus on composition and revision, some of which are noted in the Appendix.

Composition

Composition, according to the *Merriam-Webster Dictionary,* is:

> **1 a:** the act or process of composing; *specifically*: arrangement into specific proportion or relation and especially into artistic form.

Applying this definition to the writing process, composition is the process of arranging words into an artistic form. It takes skill to do this, and just as a person develops skills in piano playing or football, you need to practice the basics of writing in order to begin mastering the skills. After putting ideas down in an initial draft, writers generally work on improving the composition aspect of writing. That is, the writer refines and polishes it to get the rough edges off. In this way, the reader can focus on the overall meaning, rather than on specific word choices, sentence structure, or grammatical issues.

Content, Organization, and Tone

One area of composition that the CAPT Writing Across the Disciplines assesses is how well you can improve content (the topic, subtopic, and details you put into a piece of writing), organization (as discussed in detail in Chapters 3 and 5), and tone (choosing words and phrases that are appropriate to your purpose and audience). The Editing and Revising test specifically addresses several aspects of this area.

Topic Sentence

The topic sentence is the main idea of a paragraph. You may have been taught in the past that it is usually the first sentence, but that is not always the case. A topic sentence may actually appear in any part of a paragraph. However, there are certain things you can do to find the topic sentence of a paragraph:

- Look for the general statement. The most general statement will probably be the topic sentence. Its job is to make sure you have a basic idea of what the paragraph is discussing and it will probably not be as specific as some of the other sentences.
- Look for the most definitive statement. The statement that makes a point or establishes a point the writer wants to show as fact is the stronger sentence, and will very likely be the sentence that all the others explain and support.
- Separate out the sentences that contain the details. The topic sentence will most likely not contain specific details. It is generally the job of the other sentences to bolster the topic sentence. The details support it. If you think of a paragraph as a pyramid, the topic sentence will be at the top, and all the other sentences will be on the lower levels, supporting the main idea.
- Look for the statement that every other statement in the paragraph relates back to. In one way or another, each of the other sentences in a paragraph should refer back to the topic sentence. The supporting statements may not relate directly to each other, but they will all relate to the main idea.

Let's take a look at a couple of sample paragraphs. Try to pinpoint the topic sentence after you read each example.

Example 1

If you are a new student at our school, you are very lucky. The people at our school are extremely friendly. Many of them will offer to help you if you are lost, invite you to join a club or sport, or tell you which teachers to avoid. The other day, I saw two juniors walking with a freshman to class, giving him suggestions for which stairways to use to get to certain classes more quickly. Not everyone is so outgoing or helpful, but the majority of us are willing to do what we can to make the transition easier for the newcomer.

Example 2

I broke my finger playing basketball last summer. My friend broke her ankle playing miniature golf. A tennis ball hit another friend of mine on the head, and he got a concussion from it. Many sports can be dangerous when we do not pay close attention to what we and other participants are doing.

In the first example, the second sentence ("The people at our school are extremely friendly.") is the topic sentence. It is the most definitive, and the most general statement, with no specific details or examples. Also, each of the other sentences tells us about specific actions students have taken to be helpful or outgoing toward one another. Finally, each of the other sentences can be directly connected to that one statement.

The second example is a bit different. The first three sentences give examples of specific injuries received while playing sports. They do not directly relate to one another, but they do all support the final sentence. The final statement also makes a definitive proclamation: sports can be dangerous. Based on this analysis, the last sentence is the topic sentence.

Supporting Details

To find sentences that serve as supporting details to the topic sentence, you can

- look for the sentences with details or examples.
- look for the sentences that do not necessarily declare something as final or true. The details may be suggestive, but they are not as strong as the topic sentence.
- look for the sentences that support the topic sentence. These are the ones that are not required for the pyramid to hold up the main idea. If you pull out one or another of the sentences with supporting detail, the other sentences could rearrange themselves in the pyramid to continue supporting the main idea.
- look for the sentences that are directly related to the topic sentence. The supporting sentences may not necessarily directly relate to one another, but they will each refer to the topic sentence.

Go back to the examples above and note the supporting details. They are all in the sentences that back up the main idea, or further explain it. They may not all be directly related to each other, but they all help to give support to the topic sentence.

Extraneous (or Unnecessary) Material

Paragraphs with extraneous material are confusing and serve only to distract the reader. Information that is not relevant to the main idea of the writing in general or the paragraph in particular decreases the effectiveness of your writing. Sometimes it is hard to get rid of the extraneous information because you wrote it so well or it contains an interesting fact. However, your main idea is the focus, and no matter how wonderful the wording you created or amazing the fact, you need to get rid of it if it does not help explain your topic.

For example, it would not help to tell about a friendly person you met at the mall in Example 1. Your main idea is friendly people at school, not the mall. Similarly, it would be confusing to put the rules for basketball in Example 2 because it just would not make sense if you are explaining your theory that games can be dangerous.

Using the following examples, try to identify the information that is extraneous, or irrelevant to the rest of the paragraph.

Example 3

I found a starfish on my vacation. It was on the beach, probably washed in by the tide. It is in very good shape, with no holes or broken pieces. I went to the ice cream shop after I found the starfish. I might decide to give the starfish to my grandmother, who collects them, but it's so pretty I might just keep it on my desk.

Example 4

The stars were very bright last night. I could see many constellations, such as the big and little dippers, from my backyard. I guess there were no clouds to hide them from me. I heard an owl too, which was really cool. I like studying the constellations and examining the skies. Someday, I'd like to travel in space to see them from a new perspective.

In Example 3, the sentence about having ice cream does not really fit with the rest of the paragraph. While it refers to the starfish, it does not tell us anything about the starfish or the author's reflection about finding the starfish. In Example 4, the paragraph is about watching the skies, and while the author may have heard an owl at the same time she saw the stars, that information does not fit.

Chronological and Logical Order

Your paragraphs and your writing as a whole need to be in an order that makes sense. Order may be based on chronology, topic, or importance. It can also be based on size (e.g., mouse, cat, horse, moose) or distance (New York City, Alaska, Japan). In fact, you can order your writing in any way that is logical in terms of the topic you have chosen.

An examination of a couple of lists of topics and subtopics will help you understand the idea of order. Try to establish how you might order them, whether within a paragraph or a whole piece of writing:

Example 5

World War II
Gulf War
Vietnam War
World War I

In this example, the writer is considering something about different wars. One way to organize it logically would be to put the paragraphs in chronological order. To do this, you would start with the earliest war, World War I. The sequence would continue with World War II, Vietnam, and the Gulf War.

Example 6

Streets
Highways
Sidewalks
Paths

This example examines the types of tracks or courses people use for transportation. One way to order the paragraphs or sentences logically would be to discuss them from smallest to largest: paths, sidewalks, streets, highways. Other ways to order them would depend on the nature of the discussion about these places. A paper on the level and types of danger for the pedestrian might use this order: streets, highways, paths, sidewalks. There is not always just one way to order topics, but sometimes the focus of a paper will dictate the most logical, or best, order.

Tone

Your writing can express attitude, either positive or negative, by the way you phrase your sentences, the words you choose, and the manner in which you address your audience. In most writing you will do for school, work, or tests such as the CAPT, use a formal, respectful tone. Avoid using slang, unless your topic is directly related to such words. Using words that are obscure or extremely technical can make your writing appear arrogant. Being too simplistic, on the other hand, can give the reader the impression that you do not have a depth of understanding about your topic. In working with tone, you need to think about your feelings about your topic and about your audience so your writing will reflect your intent.

As you think about tone, consider the fact that excessive repetition of your ideas within paragraphs and throughout your work can bore your reader. Repeating the same idea in different ways can make your work seem superficial and your knowledge weak. Try to say something clearly and concisely once, and then do not repeat it unless you are examining it more closely or comparing it to another idea. Here is an example of a paragraph with redundancy:

Example 7

People who litter should be subject to more severe punishments. People do not care about a $50.00 fine, and they know the police will probably not stop them for something so small. If the fines were larger, such as several hundred dollars, people would care more. They don't care so much about $50.00 because it's not a lot of money these days. If it cost more to pay a fine for a littering ticket, then more people would probably be more careful about not doing it.

If you read the paragraph carefully, you will see that the last two sentences repeat the second and third sentences. The ideas they express are not any different, and the information in those last sentences do not provide any further clarification or detail that is necessary for understanding. As such, they are redundant and reduce the clarity of the paragraph.

The composition, or the artistry, of your writing is affected by your understanding of main and supporting ideas, relevant and redundant ideas, order, and tone. Any one of these aspects of your writing can enhance your paper if used effectively, or undermine your purpose if used inappropriately.

If you struggle with these skills, you can practice identifying the topic and supporting sentences, logical order, and tone by reading material you find in magazines and newspapers. You can also try to pick out extraneous or irrelevant material or redundant ideas from such articles. Try to practice identifying composition factors in your own writing, such as reflections you do for homework, journal entries, and essays.

Sentence Structure and Syntax

Another element of composition, or revision, is syntax—how well you formulate sentences to express your thoughts clearly and appropriately given the rules of our language. Primary concerns in syntax on the CAPT are: sentence fragments, run-ons, awkward construction, parallel structure, and compound sentences.

Complete Sentences

Complete sentences, or independent clauses, must have a subject (what the sentence is about) and a predicate (generally, what the subject is doing), and express a complete thought. Complete sentences can stand on their own. While other sentences may help to explain them, complete sentences do not *require* further explanation.

Sentence Fragments

Incomplete sentences, or fragments, either do not have a subject or predicate, or they are in the form of a dependent clause. A dependent clause contains a subject and verb, but does not express a complete thought. Sentences that start with conjunctions (and, but, or) or prepositional phrases (in, through, under) are examples of sentence fragments. Unless they are dependent clauses that are connected to an independent clause with a comma, they do not stand on their own.

Figure 7.1 provides examples of fragments (in this case, dependent clauses) and how they can become part of a complete sentence.

Figure 7.1: Fragment Samples

Fragment	Complete Sentence
Breaking into many pieces.	The mirror fell, breaking into many pieces.
Under the bridge, on the path, and beside the railroad tracks.	I saw dandelions blooming under the bridge, on the path, and beside the railroad tracks.
Following her down the road.	Her puppy was following her down the road.
But I was not going to do that.	My drink would spill if I knocked it over, but I was not going to do that.
Through the fence.	Through the fence, I could see the new pony.

Compare the fragments in the first column to the complete sentences in the second. Determine what is missing from the fragment and then figure out why the added words in the second column create complete sentences. Figure 7.2 explains the problem with each fragment and corrects the fragment to make a complete sentence.

Figure 7.2: Fragment Solutions

Fragment	Complete Sentence
Breaking into many pieces. *(This fragment does not tell you what was breaking.)*	The mirror fell, breaking into many pieces.
Under the bridge, on the path, and beside the railroad tracks. *(This fragment does not tell you what was under, on, or beside the places identified.)*	I saw dandelions blooming under the bridge, on the path, and beside the railroad tracks.
Following her down the road. *(This fragment does not tell who or what was following.)*	Her puppy was following her down the road.
But I was not going to do that. *(This fragment does not stand alone because it begins with a dependent conjunction, which indicates that it should be connected to another thought.)*	My drink would spill if I knocked it over, but I was not going to do that.
Through the fence. *(This is a prepositional phrase; there is no subject or verb to tell us what or who is doing what through the fence.)*	Through the fence, I could see the new pony.

Run-ons

Another syntax error results when you add two independent sentences together without proper punctuation or connecting words. The following are examples of run-on sentences.

I was jumping up and down I twisted my ankle.

Taking my old books, I headed to the library the librarian gave me new ones.

These sentences contain more than one complete thought and must be separated into two sentences, or one of the complete thoughts needs to be turned into a dependent clause. For example:

> I was jumping up and down, and I twisted my ankle.

> Taking my old books, I headed to the library. The librarian gave me new ones.

This type of syntax error may be one of the most significant in terms of undermining your ability to write with credibility, and could impact whether a job application results in an interview, a college application is further considered, or a company takes your concerns about its product's safety seriously. Many students, even in high school, still struggle with fragments and run-ons. To avoid such errors, read your sentences out loud, review your notes or appropriate sections of a grammar book, or ask your teacher or parents for extra help.

Awkward Construction

A third syntax error has to do with awkward construction, or sentences that are written in a confusing manner. Sentences with awkward construction usually have phrases that explain other parts of the sentence in confusing places. Remember, put descriptive phrases, such as prepositional phrases, as close as possible to what they are describing. Otherwise, your sentence can be very confusing to the reader. Figure 7.3 provides examples of awkward construction.

Figure 7.3: Awkward Construction

Awkward Construction	Problem	Fixed Construction
I don't know without your help how I could finish harvesting my vegetables.	In this sentence, the "without your help" seems to refer to what the writer does not know. He probably really intends to state that he couldn't harvest his vegetables without his friend's help.	I don't know how I could finish harvesting my vegetables without your help.
I watched the climber slowly creep up the rock, petrified.	This sentence does not reveal whether it is the climber, the writer, or the rock that is petrified.	Petrified, I watched the climber slowly creep up the rock. OR I watched the petrified climber slowly creep up the rock. OR I watched the climber slowly creep up the petrified rock.

Other types of awkward sentences are simply too long and complex. A sure way to tell if you have an awkward sentence is if you have to reread it several times for it to make sense (assuming you know all of the vocabulary), or if you stumble over your words when you try to read it aloud. The best way to correct this type of awkward sentence is to divide it into smaller components. Here is an example of an awkward sentence:

> I wanted to go to the store, which is four miles away, but I
> couldn't use the car even though it was supposed to be my turn
> because it was in the shop to get the transmission, tires, and steering
> fixed since none of that had been done in a long time.

The sentence is so long that the reader begins to lose track of the point the writer is trying to make. One way to fix this awkwardness is to break the sentence into at least two, and maybe three new sentences.

> I wanted to go to the store, which is four miles away. However,
> I couldn't use the car, even though it was my turn, because it was in
> the shop. The transmission, tires, and steering all needed to be fixed
> since none of that had been done in a long time.

The best way to avoid or correct awkward sentence construction is to read what you have written and make sure it is clear. If it is not, simplify or reorganize the sentence.

Parallel Structure

Whenever you create a list or series within a sentence, you need to use similar word patterns to achieve fluency and balance. Using the same structure and style of phrases equalizes each item. You need to be careful to use parallel structure in the following areas.

Gerunds

Gerunds are verbs that end in –*ing* and act as nouns. Here is an example:

> Talking excessively was a problem of hers.
> (Gerund)

The original verb is "talk," but adding the –*ing* to the end of it permits the writer to use it as a noun in this sentence. The subject of the sentence is "talking." A gerund may also take the role of the object of the sentence or prepositional phrase. (Remember, an object of a sentence is the "who" or "what" that is being acted upon by the subject.)

Infinitives

Infinitives are verbs in their simplest form. Generally, all other forms of a verb are modifications from this basic form. The infinitive adds the word "to" in front of the verb form, for instance: "to give," "to question," "to thank." An infinitive may act as a subject, direct object, or a modifier (adverb or adjective). For example:

> She wanted <u>to talk</u> to him. (The infinitive "to talk" is acting as the direct object.)

> She went to the store <u>to buy</u> a car. ("To buy" is an infinitive acting as an adverb, describing the purpose of "went.")

To ensure parallel structure with gerunds and infinitives, make sure you consistently use one or the other, and do not mix them within the sentence or clause. For example, look at the following sentence.

> She likes <u>putting</u> on make-up, <u>fussing</u> over her hair, and
>   (Gerund)   (Gerund)
>
> <u>to dress</u> nicely.
> (Infinitive)

This sentence is not parallel because it uses two gerunds and one infinitive in the same list. To correct the sentence, you can either change each item in the list to all gerunds, or all infinitives.

> She likes <u>putting</u> on make-up, <u>fussing</u> over her hair, and
>   (Gerund)   (Gerund)
>
> <u>dressing</u> nicely.
> (Gerund)

OR

> She likes <u>to put</u> on make-up, <u>fuss</u> over her hair, and <u>dress</u> nicely.
>   (Infinitive)   (Infinitive)   (Infinitive)

Note in the second correction, the word "to" is not repeated before each verb form. While you may choose to do so, it is not necessary, since each one refers back to the original "to."

Adverbs and Adjectives

You will recall that adverbs modify verbs, adjectives or other adverbs. Adjectives modify nouns and pronouns. When using them in a list, be sure to use one or the other to ensure that you are modifying the same aspect of your sentence with the entire list. Here is an example of a sentence with adverbs and a prepositional phrase.

> Sometimes she dances around the house <u>joyfully</u>,
>   (adverb)
>
> <u>energetically</u>, and <u>in a graceful manner</u>.
> (adverb)   (prepositional phrase)

The writer started this list with two adverbs describing how she dances, but ends with a prepositional phrase that uses an adjective to modify "manner" instead of an adverb to modify "dance." To correct this, the writer could state:

Sometimes she dances around the house <u>joyfully</u>,
(adverb)

<u>energetically</u>, and <u>gracefully</u>.
(adverb)   (adverb)

The key to avoiding problems with parallel structure is to make sure that items in a list all take on the same format. If you struggle with this, take the listed items out of the sentence and rewrite them on a piece of scrap paper. Look at them closely and determine what you can do to them to make them parallel. Most of the time, it is a matter of simply changing the form of one or two words so that they match the others in the list.

Compound Sentences

The last syntax problem that the CAPT Revising and Editing test assesses is whether you can combine sentences appropriately and accurately. Most often, you will want to combine sentences when you have a series of very short, simple sentences, or you have two very closely related sentences. When you have a series of very short, simple sentences, the rhythm of your writing can become stilted, or choppy, and monotonous. For example:

I had a kitten named Persia. I let him sleep on a blanket in my
windowsill. He was limping one day. He didn't want to be touched.
I talked to him a bit and fed him. He seemed to be better the next day.

This paragraph sounds rather like a children's story, which, if that is your intent, is not terrible. However, if you are writing to someone who can process information at a higher level, you will want to add some variety to your wording. To establish a more natural rhythm, you need to vary the length and complexity of your sentences. If you were to combine these sentences to make a more interesting version of your story, you might do the following:

I had a kitten named Persia, who slept on a blanket in my
windowsill. One day he was limping and did not want to be
touched. So, I just talked to him and fed him. Luckily, the
next day he seemed to be better.

Compare the two versions of the story. Notice how the first version is choppy. Each sentence is short and simple in structure, following the same basic pattern: subject-verb-object or modifier. The second version is a bit more interesting because the sentences are more varied in composition. Turning some of the sentences into dependent clauses puts emphasis on the other sentences and establishes a more musical rhythm with ups and downs that you hear when you read it.

Another reason to combine sentences is when they are very closely related. There are several ways to do this, some of which we discussed above under the discussion on run-ons.

- **Subordination**—In the example about the cat named Persia, we took some of the simple sentences and made them into dependent clauses. While the information is still important, we made these ideas *subordinate* to other information. For example, in the first sentence of the revised paragraph, the emphasis is on the fact that the writer has a cat named Persia. The subordinate thought is that the cat sleeps on a blanket in the windowsill.
- **Repeated subjects or verbs**—If this is the case, you can combine those sentences that share the subject or verb of the prior or subsequent thoughts. For example:

> The dog ran into the fence. The dog was chasing a ball. The dog
> looked a little confused.

To fix this, you could put all the predicates together into one sentence using the same subject, which is "The dog":

> The dog looked a little confused because he was chasing a ball and
> ran into a fence.

Here is an example of a repetitive verb, followed by the corrected version:

> The dog was confused. The dog's owner was confused. The neighbor,
> who had been hit in the head with the ball, was confused.

> The dog, his owner, and the neighbor who had been hit in the head
> by the ball were all confused.

Note that in this example, the sentences all had different subjects, but the verb was the same: "was confused." The revised version places the subjects together, modifies the verb to make it plural, and creates a single, new sentence with less repetition.

- **Equality of importance**—If you need to emphasize two ideas equally, and do not want to subordinate one of the thoughts, and cannot combine them through a common subject or verb, you can use a semicolon along with a coordinating conjunction, such as "and" or "or." Each side of the semicolon must be an independent clause. For example:

> The cat was chasing the rat; however, the dog was not far behind the cat.

In this example, the writer wanted to give equal importance to the rat's and the cat's troubles. Each phrase is an independent clause—they can both stand by themselves as a complete thought. However, the thought is more complete by showing within one sentence that the cat was not only doing the chasing, but also was the one being chased by the dog.

Syntax in composition can be very tricky and confusing. The most efficient way to learn it, and to learn it well, is to practice reading and writing. Through reading literature and essays written by strong writers, you will reinforce your own internal rhythm and increase your natural tendency to write with few syntax problems. By practicing writing and revising with your own thoughts, you can develop an eye for your strengths and weaknesses so that you know what you need to work on each time you are required to write a formal assignment. The important idea is that you do not give up on the process of developing strong skills in syntax. It is not impossible, but it does take work to understand it and use it well.

Word Choice

A third area of composition, or revision, that the CAPT test assesses is how well you choose your words. The key to word selection is to be as precise and vivid as possible to express your ideas in a compelling yet clear manner. You use your words to draw in your readers and to keep them interested in your writing.

Descriptive Language

Descriptive language is required if you want the reader to be able to truly imagine what you are discussing in your writing. You could state that the tree in your yard is scary, or you can really frighten your reader by using more descriptive language to bring it to life. Descriptive language appeals to the five senses (sound, sight, touch, taste, smell). If you want the reader to understand what you experienced holding a kitten, describe what you felt and heard. For instance, explain that the kitten was softer than a cotton ball and lighter than a piece of paper, or that the mew was gentle and curious. Paint the picture so the reader can experience your words, rather than just read them. Compare the following sentences:

> Daphne studied the lake, wishing she could be out on the sailboat.

> Daphne studied the quiet ripples of the water in the lake, wishing she too could be out on the gently bobbing sailboat.

The first sentence lets you know Daphne wants to be on the boat. The descriptive language in the second sentence gives you a sense of why Daphne wants to be on the boat. You can sense her mood and the effect of the lake on her state of mind. Descriptive language helps bring alive Daphne's desire to be on the lake.

Transition Words

Transition words improve the flow of your writing. They help the reader switch gears as they move from one thought to the next. You can use transition words between paragraphs or between sentences. The most effective transitions refer to the prior subject and introduce the next with the use of transition words and phrases. A few of the more common transitional words and phrases include:

In addition to	On the other hand
However	Sometimes
Further	In summary
Even though	Likewise

When you use a transition properly, you connect your ideas together and hint at what you are going to tell the reader next. The transition words explain how the ideas are connected, either by time, importance, addition, or comparison or contrast. Here is an example.

Martha wanted to see what the man was going to do next, so she quietly followed him toward Adams Street. He looked over his shoulder several times, but he did not appear to notice her. She tried to stay several paces behind, and in the shadows of the trees. Once they arrived on Adams Street, the man entered the pawnshop. Even though Martha was nervous that he noticed her on the street, she went into the store too.

In this example, the transition, "once," occurs between the description of Martha following the man along the street to the movement into the store. The transition lets the reader know that the next sentences will explain what happens inside the pawnshop and pulls the reader into a new thought pattern. The following is an example of a transition between sentences within a paragraph.

Jason was a very good student in math. However, his grades in English were much lower.

In this example, the transition shows a contrast between the student's skills in math and English. The word "however" indicates that the next idea is related to the first, but is going to be of a different nature. By using such transitional words, a writer can help improve the artistry, or composition, of the piece and provide clarity for the reader.

Specificity

Being specific in word choice will help you achieve clarity. The more specific the words you choose in your writing, the more clearly the reader will understand what you are discussing. For example, you can write about the neighbor's dog, and indicate to the reader that it is a four-legged creature that barks. However, if you are more specific, such as stating that the dog is a St. Bernard, you will help the reader visualize the size and color of the dog. Your writing composition will be more polished when you use more specific words.

Modifiers

Modifiers that are placed properly also add clarity to your writing. Modifiers are adjectives and adverbs that work best when they are placed as close to the word they are modifying as they possibly can be. Compare the following sentences.

> The student's <u>misshapen</u> painting was a woman.
> (modifier)

> The student's painting was a <u>misshapen</u> woman.
> (modifier)

As you can see, the placement of the modifier is important in helping the reader to understand what you are trying to say. In the first sentence, the painting is misshaped, indicating that the canvas might be warped. In the second, the woman the student painted was misshaped.

Some words can give writers particular problems if they are not used carefully. For instance, compare the following sentences.

> I <u>almost</u> rode all of the rides at the fair.
> (problematic modifier)

OR

> I rode <u>almost</u> all of the rides at the fair.
> (problematic modifier)

In the first version, the writer did not actually get on the rides; he almost did. In the second version, he rode on most, but not all of the rides. Other words that tend to cause this problem include: *just, only, hardly, mostly*, and *always*. Be careful that you place these modifiers so that your meaning is clear. Also, the words "always" and "never" should be used with caution; they are extremes that rarely occur.

Misplaced modifiers can also take the form of a phrase. For example:

> <u>Hopping away</u>, the boy watched the rabbit.
> (misplaced modifier)

From this sentence, it appears that the boy was hopping away. There are a couple of ways to correct this type of modifier problem. Possible corrections include:

> Hopping away, the rabbit escaped the boy who watched him.

OR

> The boy watched the rabbit hopping away.

Sometimes, we mistakenly exclude what we are intending to modify. The modifier in the following sentence is said to be dangling. It is dangling because it has nothing to modify. Here is an example:

> Quitting for lunch, the work was left behind.

We know that the work probably was not doing the quitting, but the reader does not know who or what was. To correct this, you need to explain what is being described:

> Quitting for lunch, the secretaries left their work behind.

OR

> The secretaries left their work behind when they quit for lunch.

The key to correctly placing modifiers is figuring out what is being modified and then placing the modifiers as close as possible to what they are modifying. If necessary, break the sentence into pieces, separating out the subject, the verb, and the object. Then, determine what the modifier appears to explain further. Once you have figured it out, put the sentence back together with the modifier as close to the part of the sentence that it clarifies.

Faulty Subordination and Coordination

As you know, subordination is the process of making one idea less important to another by putting it into the form of a dependent clause and connecting it to an independent clause. This creates a complex sentence. Coordination is the process of connecting two ideas that are of equal importance in a compound sentence.

To avoid problems with faulty coordination, you need to be sure that you give equal weight to both parts of the sentence. Each independent clause needs to maintain its independence. To do this, you separate the clauses by a comma and join them together by one of the following coordinating conjunctions: *and, or, either, but, so, for, nor, yet.*

Do not minimize the importance of one sentence by turning it into a dependent clause with a conjunction other than one of the seven coordinating conjunctions. Also, remember that a conjunction is not a necessary element to either clause, but helps to explain how the two are connected. You could remove the conjunction and separate the clauses into two sentences without affecting the meaning. If you tried this with a subordinate clause, however, you could lose meaning such as time, place, cause and effect, or comparison or contrast.

To avoid problems with faulty subordination, make sure that the subordinate, or dependent, clause is less important than the independent clause in relation to the rest of the paragraph or main idea. Also, you use a comma only if the dependent clause precedes the independent clause. For example:

> <u>When she took her shoes off</u>, she discovered a blister on her heel.
>   (dependent clause)   (independent clause)

OR

> She discovered a blister on her heel <u>when she took her shoes off</u>.
>   (independent clause)   (dependent clause)

Note that there is no comma when the dependent clause follows the independent clause. This is because the idea that she took her shoes off is subordinate to the fact that she has a blister. The sentence is not as effective if the importance were switched:

> She took her shoes off, and she found a blister.

The fact that she took her shoes off does not carry the same importance as the blister. Depending on the nature of the story, the blister will probably have a greater effect on what happens to her later than the fact that she took her shoes off. The blister can affect her mood, her willingness to do something, or even whether she will wear sandals or shoes when she has to run to catch a bus.

In choosing words to reflect proper subordination, you need to select a conjunction that reflects how the dependent clause relates to the independent, more important clause. As indicated above, such meaning will relate to time (when, until, before, after), place (wherever), cause or effect (because, since), or comparison or contrast (similarly, even though).

Summary of Revision

There are many aspects of our language that you need to consider in the artistry of writing. As you revise your work and turn it into a composition that shines, you need to remember several things, including content, organization, tone, syntax, and word choice. The likelihood of being tested on each and every one of these areas on your CAPT exam is very low. However, you need to be prepared to handle a question from each of these aspects of composition. In addition to practicing these skills, Chapter 9 offers some test-taking skills that can help you be successful on this test.

Chapter 8:
Editing Your Writing

Editing is an important aspect of the writing process. At this stage, you polish your writing by correcting grammatical or usage errors. While revision focuses on how you compose your words, editing focuses on the grammar rules, including capitalization, punctuation, usage (parts of speech), and spelling.

Capitalization

When to capitalize the first letter of a word is probably the skill you have been working on the longest. Generally, you need to capitalize a word when it deserves a certain level of importance. For instance, you always capitalize the first word in a sentence to make sure that it clearly shows where a new thought begins. The CAPT Editing and Revising test will make sure that you properly capitalize in five areas.

1. **Titles of people**—Capitalize words that are titles that appear before a person's name, such as Dr., Mr., Ms., and Mrs. Also, capitalize job titles that appear before a person's name: President Johnson, Congresswoman Smith, Queen Elizabeth. Family relationships are also capitalized when they appear before a name: Uncle John, Grandma Stevens, or Cousin Lisa.
2. **Proper nouns**—Words that identify a specific place, event, time period, or language are considered proper nouns, and must be capitalized. Examples include: California, Atlantic Ocean, World War II, Cuban Missile Crisis, Industrial Revolution, Reconstruction, and Spanish.
3. **Proper adjectives**—Certain proper nouns that act as adjectives must be capitalized. For instance, when describing something from a specific location, you would capitalize the adjective but not the noun; e.g., German chocolate cake, Persian rug,

or Southern hospitality. Other proper adjectives are brand names that are used to describe the specific object you are discussing. For example: Kleenex tissues, Panasonic television, or Hershey's candy.

4. **First word in dialogue**—When writing dialogue, you always capitalize the first word, whether it starts the sentence or not. This is because it represents the initial thought of the speaker. For example: *The teacher further explained, "When you add these chemicals together, they become stronger."*

5. **Names**—Most names, whether they identify a person, place, or thing, are considered proper nouns; however, some can be confusing. In addition to those already addressed, the state has also identified in the *Connecticut Academic Performance Test Second Generation Reading and Writing Across the Disciplines Handbook* the following proper nouns:

Organizations:	American Cancer Society, Union Local 111
Buildings:	Frank Muir Building, White House
Works of art:	*The Scream, Mona Lisa*

Capitalization is rather straightforward. If you cannot determine that a word defines something specific and important, or does not begin a sentence or dialogue, it most likely does not get capitalized.

Punctuation

You can probably name several types of punctuation, and are relatively clear on how to use most of them. Since you started writing sentences in elementary school, you have been working with the period, question mark, and exclamation point. You have also worked with other punctuation, such as the comma, colon, and semicolon. These, however, have some trickier rules. The punctuation that the CAPT focuses on includes the comma, quotation marks, the apostrophe, the semicolon, and the colon. The way the CAPT Editing and Revising test might assess you on their uses is discussed below.

Commas

The comma is used to separate sentences into smaller parts. The comma helps explain the association of phrases and words to each other within the sentence. Commas can be used in several ways, six of which are assessed on the CAPT.

1. **Separating words and phrases in a series**—The comma goes after each item, except the last. For example:

The animals included bears, mountain cats, and raccoons.

The little boy made a snowball, threw it at the tree, and accidentally hit a bird.

There was a time in the 1980s and early 1990s when some people decided the comma before the last item was not necessary. However, that view is changing again. The last comma serves to clarify that the last two items are distinct from each other and carry the same weight as each of the rest of the items.

2. **Separating clauses in compound sentences**—This is discussed in Chapter 7, under the discussion of compound sentences—joining two independent clauses with a coordinating conjunction (and, or, yet, nor, but, so, either). The comma appears immediately after the first independent clause, and just before the coordinating conjunction.

3. **Writing dates**—The following are examples of how commas should be used when writing a date. Note that a comma comes after the day of the month and the year when writing out a full date.

    He was born on July 16, 1965, in Watertown.

    The accident occurred at this intersection in October 1987.

4. **Setting an introductory phrase apart from the rest of a sentence**—This phrase is usually a dependent clause or a prepositional or adverbial phrase. It serves to provide context for the sentence, but is not an essential element. It sets the background for the noun and verb phrases. For example:

    When I was young, I called her Grandma Mom.
    (introductory phrase)

    In the middle of the night, the bike fell over and scared us.
    (introductory phrase)

    Looking out the door, she saw a moose in the backyard.
    (introductory phrase)

5. **Setting off appositives: words or phrases that are used to clarify or identify another word, usually a noun**—You must always use a comma before and after an appositive, unless the appositive begins or ends the sentence. Examples are:

    The guy next door, Marcus, amused all of the children with his antics.
    (appositive)

    Carly, my cousin's daughter, is very cute.
    (appositive)

    Margery worked hard to exercise, strengthening and stretching, her
    (appositive)
    injured shoulder.

6. **Setting off parenthetical expressions**—A parenthetical expression is an unnecessary phrase. If it is removed, the basic meaning of the sentence is not lost. It may serve as clarification or explanation. Sometimes, a parenthetical will interrupt the flow of the sentence because it might appear to change the direction of the thought. For this reason, a parenthetical is always set off with commas. Here are some examples:

> He was reading that book, <u>the one on the chair</u>, before he went to bed.
> (parenthetical phrase)

> The cows were in the road, <u>the third time this month</u>, and
> (parenthetical phrase)
> had to be put in the barn while the fence was being fixed.

> He wanted to go somewhere, <u>anywhere</u>, and collect his thoughts.
> (parenthetical)

There are many other uses for commas that are not included in this discussion; however, the state of Connecticut doesn't generally test for them. Some comma uses not mentioned here are more common and simple, and you should be using them easily at this point. Others are more complex, and you are not expected to have a strong grasp of them yet. Again, if you are struggling with the six areas of comma usage identified in this chapter, get extra help or refer to a grammar book.

Quotation Marks

When you are using someone else's words or writing a fictional dialogue, you need to show the reader that you are doing so by using quotation marks. The quotation marks appear before the first quoted word and after the last.

> Janet said, "I wanted to read that book, but I haven't had the time."

You should set the quote apart from the rest of the sentence with a comma (see above example), or with a colon if the quote is preceded by an independent clause.

> Sometimes her statements were incorrect: "Seventy times three
> is ninety."

As discussed above under capitalization, you capitalize the first letter of the first word in the quote. However, if the quote is separated within the sentence by other words, you do not capitalize the first word of the second part of the quote.

> "I liked watching that movie," she said, "because it was scary."

Apostrophes

The apostrophe is used to denote ownership, indicate missing letters, or note the plural of a single letter of the alphabet. When using the apostrophe to denote ownership, you put it between the noun and the letter *s,* if the noun is singular.

> The banana's color is yellow.
> (singular noun)

> Peter's shoes were untied.
> (singular noun)

If the person or thing that "owns" is plural and ends in an "s," the apostrophe appears after the *s.*

> The bosses' cars were all scratched.
> (plural noun)

> All of the kids' mittens were wet.
> (plural noun)

BUT

> All of the children's mittens were wet.
> (singular noun)

Notice that the words "bosses" and "kids" are plural, so the apostrophes follows the s. *However,* the word "children," although it is a plural noun, it doesn't end in *s.* Therefore, it takes the singular form with the apostrophe appearing before the *s.*

We also use the apostrophe to form contractions or otherwise indicate some missing letters. For example, when you combine the words "do" and "not," you use the apostrophe to show that you have removed the "o" to make the word *don't.* If you are writing dialogue and want to represent the dialect of a certain group, you can use an apostrophe. For example, the word "helping" could be shown as *helpin'* to reflect that the speaker drops his or her g's.

One of the most confusing aspects of the apostrophe involves the use of *its* and *it's.* In this case of *its,* no apostrophe is used to denote ownership, as in "Its favorite food is bananas." On the other hand, the apostrophe is used to indicate the missing letter *i,* when combining the words *it* and *is* to create the contraction *it's.*

The final use of the apostrophe is to discuss the letters of the alphabet. When you need to refer to a letter of the alphabet, it is clearer if you use the apostrophe followed by the letter "*s.*" This use helps to prevent confusion about the writer's meaning.

> All of his g's were backward.

> Her l's sounded funny.

Semicolons

The semicolon is used to connect two independent clauses that are so closely related that you do not want them to be separate sentences.

My shoes are really cool; they have ribbons instead of shoelaces.

The weather has been really bad lately; all it has done is rain.

The semicolon is also used to separate items in a rather long or otherwise complex list.

She stored lots of things in her tree house, including: blankets, pillows, and towels; books, notebooks, and pens; and toys and games.

Colons

The colon is a more definitive stopping point than a semicolon, but not as strong as a period. A colon is used to introduce a lengthy list, whether or not the items in the list are separated by commas or by semicolons. (See the example directly above.)

Colons are also used to place emphasis on a word, phrase, or clause that explains the preceding independent clause. For example:

Her identity was based on one thing: appearance.

The animals were starving: They had started to move closer to the roads to find food.

These punctuation skills, like any other grammar skills, can be reinforced with practice through reading and writing. If you need help finding specific ways to practice, ask your teacher or refer to a grammar book.

Usage

Usage is the proper use of some of the parts of speech: verbs (agreement and tense), pronouns (reference and case), and adjectives/adverbs. Other usage with respect to parts of speech are, like commas, basic enough that you are sure to know them, or so complex that you are not yet expected to know all the rules.

Subject-Verb Agreement

It is very important that your verbs agree in number with your subject. If you are talking about two gerbils, then the verb that describes their action must be the plural form of the verb. If you describe one politician, the verb must be in the singular form. Here are two examples (in this section, the subject is in bold and the verb underlined):

The **girls** <u>walk</u> to school.

Susan <u>walks</u> to school.

If the subject is two or more nouns connected by the word "and," you must use the plural form of the verb.

Susan and Becky <u>walk</u> to school.

Susan and the other **girls** <u>walk</u> to school.

If the words "or" or "nor" connect two singular subjects, you use the singular form of the verb. However, if the subjects are singular and plural, your verb will agree with the one closest to it.

Jacob or Allie <u>wins</u> the prize ever year.

Daniel or his **parents** <u>pay</u> to fix it.

The **twins or Stephanie** <u>comes</u> to the store with me.

Verb agreement can be tricky when the subject is separated from the predicate by another phrase or clause. Pay particular attention to prepositional phrases: The object of a preposition cannot be the subject of the sentence.

The **book** on top *of the boxes* <u>is</u> really interesting.
(prepositional phrase)

The **suitcase** *with the flowers* on it, which is in the cellar, <u>breaks</u> frequently.
(prepositional phrase)

Collective nouns, such as "group," "family," and "herd," refer to a number of members. However, they take the singular verb when they are in their singular form. Generally, you only use the plural form of the verb when the collective noun itself is plural. For example:

The **team** <u>asks</u> the coach for a break every 10 minutes!

In the fall, the **gaggles** of geese usually <u>stop</u> at the bog to rest.

Team, in the first sentence, is a collective singular noun. Gaggles, however, is a collective plural noun. The first sentence refers to only one team, while the second sentence is about more than one gaggle.

Some pronouns can present problems with verb agreement. Words such as "each," "none," "either," and "neither," will take a singular verb. Plural pronouns, such as "every," "everyone," "few," and "some," require a plural verb. It is best if you memorize these exceptions.

Each of the girls <u>wants</u> to buy the dress.

Everyone <u>gives</u> a dollar to the fund.

Some of the children <u>sleep</u> on the ride home.

When choosing whether to use a singular or plural verb, the most important skill is identifying the subject of the sentence. Once you have done so, you can determine whether it is plural or singular and choose the correct verb. If you are still in doubt, choose the one that sounds correct. Our speech patterns tend to reflect this rule of the language rather accurately, and you should be able to "hear" the correct choice.

Verb Tense

Verb tense reflects the time in which an action takes place. If it is now, the verb takes the present tense. If it will happen tomorrow, it will take the future tense. If it happened yesterday, it will take the past tense. There are other tenses, such as the past continuous (i.e., action that had been happening in the past), and future perfect (i.e., an action that will have taken place).

One important matter to consider with respect to verb tense is consistency. You need to make sure that within a piece of writing, and especially within paragraphs, you use the same tense throughout. There are occasions when variation is appropriate, and perhaps even helpful, but as a rule, you should maintain the past tense throughout the paragraph if the main idea is in the past tense. What problem do you see in the following example?

> Rachel just knew the cat was lost and could not find its way home in the rain. She worries that it will never return to her. As she dressed for bed, she began to cry.

In this paragraph, the main idea is in the past tense. The second sentence, however, is in the present tense, causing a shift that disrupts the flow of the reading. In order to maintain fluency, the author should change "worries" to "worried."

Pronouns

For some reason, pronouns pose particular problems for us. We tend to get confused about subject/verb agreement, reference to antecedents, and which case to use. We also tend to struggle with how to use indefinite pronouns properly.

A pronoun is a word that refers to a noun, which is the antecedent. Using a pronoun is another way to indicate the subject of a clause without repeating the same word over and over. In the following examples, the antecedent is in bold and the pronoun is underlined:

> The **girl** took off <u>her</u> hat.

> The **students** followed <u>their</u> own rules.

> **Jennifer and Louise** lost <u>their</u> privileges.

In these examples, the noun is denoted in bold, and the pronoun is underlined. The pronoun replaces the noun in part of the sentence. Instead of telling us the students followed the student's rules, we substitute "their" for students to avoid repetitiveness. Be sure to notice that the pronoun agrees in number with its antecedent. In the examples above, "girl" and "her" are singular, and "students" and "their" are plural.

Note that in these examples, the pronoun refers directly to the noun it replaces. There is no question whose hat, rules, or privileges we are discussing. Sometimes, however, there are pronouns that are indefinite; they might refer to something general, but they do not relate back to any particular person or thing.

Indefinite pronouns that are singular, such as "every," "no one," and "each," take a singular verb. In these examples, the indefinite pronoun is in bold, and the verb is underlined:

No one <u>can</u> take the place of a mother.

Each cat <u>follows</u> its owner home.

Plural pronouns, such as "few," "every," and "both," take plural verbs.

Every day <u>is</u> a new beginning.

Both of them <u>want</u> to get a new car.

Some indefinite pronouns can be either plural or singular. Examples of such indefinite pronouns include: "all" (all of the carpet, all of the students), "none" (none of the kids, none of the tables), and "any" (any number, any of the money).

Sometimes the antecedent of the pronoun is vague. That is, there may be two or more nouns in the sentence that the pronoun may be replacing. In such instances, you need to be sure to be as specific as possible with the pronoun so that your meaning is clear. For example:

Doug knocked the television off the stand and scratched it.

In this example, you cannot tell if "it" refers to the television or the stand. Depending on your meaning, the sentence should be rewritten for clarity in one of the following ways:

Doug knocked the television off the stand. The television was scratched.

OR

Doug knocked the television off the stand, which got scratched.

OR

Doug knocked the television, which got scratched, off the stand.

Notice that the last version is more awkward because the phrase "which got scratched" tends to interfere with the focus and emphasis of the sentence. Correct such problems with an eye toward maintaining the flow and rhythm of the sentence.

Another concern with pronouns is gender agreement. If the antecedent is male, be sure the pronoun is male. If the antecedent is neutral, use a neutral pronoun. In the following examples, the word in bold is the antecedent and the underlined word is the pronoun.

> **Joe** took <u>his</u> shoes off.
> (male)

> Rachel's **novel,** with <u>its</u> torn cover, was under the bed.
> (neutral)

When the gender of the noun is indefinite and singular, be careful not to use "their," which is a plural pronoun. Either use both genders or rephrase the sentence so that you avoid the indefinite pronoun.

> **Everyone,** including Timmy, wanted to have <u>his</u> wish granted.

> **Each** student stated that <u>he or she</u> had to go to the restroom.

Another way pronouns may be assessed on your CAPT Editing and Revising test concerns what person to use: first, second, or third. First person is used when referring to yourself. Personal pronouns include the singular "I," "my," and "mine," as well as the plural "we," "us," and "ours." The second person refers to a specific other, which is the audience, in the form of "you" and "yours." The third person refers to people or things in general and not specifically to yourself or your audience. Examples of third person pronouns are: "he," "she," "it," "them," "they," and "their." Notice how the pronouns in the following sentences do not match in number, or person, to the antecedent.

> The teacher asked Joseph and Susan to stop his talking.

> Wandering away from their home, Stephanie discovered she was lost.

In order to correct these sentences, you would need to change "his" to "their" in the first example, and "their" to "her" in the second example.

A last issue to consider with pronouns is case: objective, subjective, or possessive. Possessive is probably the easiest case to consider. The possessive case denotes ownership, or possession. The possessive pronouns include: "my," "mine," "yours," "ours," "his," "her," "hers," "its," and "theirs."

> Beth went to your house to look for **your** brother.

> Ken wanted to find **his** tape before he began the project.

In the first example, the possessive pronoun "your" signifies that it was the brother of the person being spoken to that Beth wanted to find. In the second example, the possessive pronoun is "his," denoting that the tape Ken wanted was his own.

If the pronoun is being used as the subject of the sentence, you use the subjective case. Subjective pronouns include: "I," "we," "you," "he," "she," "it," and "they." Sometimes the pronoun will share its role as subject with a noun or another pronoun. In these situations, you need to be sure to still use the subjective case. For example, you would not write: "*Me and Joseph* went to the store" (incorrect usage). Rather, you would write: "*Joseph and I* went to the store" (correct usage). When in doubt, eliminate the other part of the subject and read the sentence aloud with your pronoun choice. If it sounds right, it is probably right. (You do not say "Me went to the store.")

The third and final case for pronouns is the objective case, where the pronoun is being acted upon by a verb or is the object of a preposition. These pronouns include: "me," "us," "you," "it," "him," "her," and "them."

Pronoun usage is complicated by several rules of the language. If you need further assistance with any of the areas discussed above, seek extra help or refer to a grammar book. If you are confident of your skills in the areas discussed above, take it upon yourself to investigate some of the other, more complex, rules that apply to the use of pronouns. Refer to Figure 8.1 for a visual perspective on personal pronouns.

Figure 8.1: Personal Pronoun List by Case

Person	Possessive	Subjective	Objective
1st person singular	my mine	I	me
1st person plural	ours	we	us
2nd person singular	your	you	
2nd person plural	yours	you	
3rd person singular	his hers its	he she it	him her it
3rd person plural	theirs	their	them

Adjectives and Adverbs

Adjectives modify nouns and pronouns by explaining the character, color, size, style, or other aspect of the word. Adverbs modify verbs, adjectives, or other adverbs by explaining how, when, where, why, how often, or to what extent. Adverbs often end in *–ly,* or are common words such as very or always.

There are several pairs of adverbs and adjectives that cause confusion for many people. Three of these, with the adjective listed first, are: "good/well"; "real/really"; and "sure/surely." The trick with each of these is to determine what is being modified, then determine what part of speech it is. If the word is a noun or pronoun, you should use the adjective. If it is a verb, adverb, or adjective, you need to choose the adverb. For example:

I did well on that exam. ("Well" modifies "did," a verb.)

I did a good job on that project. ("Good" modifies "job," which is a noun.)

I was sure the store was closed. ("Sure" modifies "I.")

The store was surely closed. ("Surely" modifies "closed.")

The place was really packed. ("Packed" is a verb, requiring the adverb "really.")

The banana tasted really good. ("Good" is an adjective which is modified by the adverb "really.")

The real problem was the broken glass. ("Problem," a noun, is modified by the adjective "real.")

Spelling

One last area of editing that can cause significant problems for people is spelling, especially when words sound alike but are spelled differently and have different meanings. These are called "homonyms." Here is a list of some of the most common words that people often confuse, along with their meanings, which you can study.

Figure 8.2: Commonly Misspelled Words

There: a place **Their:** ownership by more than one **They're:** contraction for "they are"	**It's:** contraction for "it is" **Its:** ownership for a neutral object
Accept: to receive willingly **Except:** exclude	**Than:** comparison, instead of **Then:** reference to time
Choose: select **Chose:** selected (past tense)	**Where:** a place **Were:** plural past tense of to be
Affect: an action (verb) **Effect:** a result	**Conscious:** to be aware **Conscience:** moral awareness
Lose: not win **Loose:** not tight, baggy	**To:** infinitive of a verb, a preposition **Too:** also **Two:** number equal to 1 + 1
Hear: perceive by ear **Here:** location	**Whether:** denotes alternatives **Weather:** temperature, precipitation
Our: personal plural pronoun **Are:** state of being	

The English language is full of rules and exceptions to the rules that probably serve more to confuse us than they do to give us a standard, conventional written language. However, society has agreed to follow these rules in order to be able to understand one another's written work. Most people remember the basic rules, those that are needed the most often, and have a reference source to rely on when they are unsure of which rule applies or how to apply it.

Now that you have reviewed many composition and revision rules, you are ready to learn about the actual test format for the Editing and Revising portion of CAPT.

Chapter 9:
Editing and Revising—The Task

The CAPT Editing and Revising assessment is a multiple-choice test. You are given three readings that have several errors in them, and you will need to correct the errors by choosing the correct response to 18 multiple-choice questions. Your raw score on this part of the Writing Across the Disciplines test is based on the number of items you answer correctly. If you give 14 correct answers, the number that goes into the formula for determining your CAPT Writing score is 14. See Chapter 1 for more information on scoring.

You have likely taken so many multiple-choice tests in your academic career that you have your own method on how to complete them efficiently. However, these tips can help you increase your chances of doing well.

You should start the test by reading the questions for the first passage before you read the passage itself. Doing so will help your brain focus on the types of errors you will be correcting so that you can notice them more readily as you read.

Read each question slowly and completely. You want to ensure that you understand the question. Do not assume that by reading the first few words you will know what you need to do. The rest of the question may change in context from what you expected.

Before you select your answer, read every choice you are given. Sometimes one of the answers pops out as correct, but you are looking for the **best** possible answer. If you read every choice, you will be less likely to miss a question that you know you could have answered correctly.

Be sure to visually or mentally test each of the possible answers in the sentence to which the question refers. If you are a visual learner, write the choices in pencil over the text in the passage so you can see the possibilities. Sometimes hearing or seeing the correct grammar or usage in context helps us to find it more easily.

Try not to guess unless you absolutely have to do so. If you do guess, eliminate as many options as you can to improve your odds in answering the question correctly. Selecting from two options gives you better odds than selecting from three or four options. After you narrow down your choices, select the one that makes the most sense. Substitute it into the context and then use these thinking strategies to help you. Does the substitution sound right? Does it sound better than the next option? Does it look similar to examples and practice items you have seen before? If you are still in doubt, go with your first instinct. Usually your intuition will tell you what is right, even when you try to over-think the problem.

Last, never change an answer unless you are absolutely sure that the change is accurate. It is too easy to talk yourself out of a correct answer when you are unsure. If you do change an answer, make sure the change is based on some information or realization that you did not consider when you made your first choice.

In addition to these strategies, you need to remember that the time given to finish this test is very short and you will be working rapidly to complete the questions. If you do finish early, go back and review as many questions as you can. Sometimes you find that you misread a question or accidentally marked an "a" response instead of a "b" response. Most of all, have faith in your knowledge and skills. Keeping these simple factors in mind should strengthen your confidence.

Chapter 10:
Final Thoughts and Encouragement

Everyone is a writer. Since you were born, you have been taking in the rules of the language; in fact, you started practicing the conventions of the English language when you began to speak it as a baby. Sometime around the age of five, you started learning how to use the language by writing it. From then on, you practiced using it in more complex and creative ways, following the rules that became ingrained by listening to your parents and other family members, friends, television characters, and teachers.

The CAPT Writing Across the Disciplines assessment is just one more way to show that you have mastered a certain level of skill in using the language. Most of the test will likely be very easy for you. In fact, one of the more significant problems students have with the test is taking it in a timed environment. The element of time can add pressure and slow down the process. If time pressure is a problem for you, practice writing for short periods of time. Eventually, build yourself up to about an hour of steady writing. This will help you to prepare for this element of the test.

There is no need to pressure yourself to get a perfect score; just do the best you can. The more subtle aspects of writing (diction, fluency, and complex grammar rules) can slip by most of us. Only a few people learn everything there is about a topic; many of us tend to learn most, but not all, of the nuances. People understand better that which they use most often, and for those rules that impact writing infrequently, dictionaries, style manuals, and thesauruses are necessary.

Finally, some suggestions were repeated throughout the entire book. Just in case you have not picked up on them, here they are again. They are very important for you to succeed, not only on CAPT, but in life.

- Be confident in yourself and your abilities; you have been doing this for years.
- When in doubt about your skill level, ask for extra help or consult an appropriate grammar or usage text.
- Practice, practice, practice. Just as you need to practice to improve your athletic skills, you need to practice to improve and reinforce your writing skills.

Use this book as a resource, a reminder, and for practice. Use your brain for success. Good luck, and whenever you can, make your work experience fun.

Appendix:
Works Consulted

Connecticut State Department of Education. "The Connecticut Academic Performance Test Second Generation Reading and Writing Across the Disciplines Handbook." 2001. July–September 2003. *http://www.state.ct.us/sde/dtl/curriculum/currlang_publ_capt.htm*

Darling, Charles. "Guide to Grammar and Writing." August 22, 1999. August–September 2003. *http://webster.commnet.edu/grammar/index.htm.*

"Grammar Guide—Grammar Station." 2002. August–September 2003. *http://www.grammarstation.com/grammarguide.*

"Grammar Slammer—English Grammar Resource." June 24, 1997. August–September 2003. *http://englishplus.com/grammar.*

McMurray, David A. "Online Technical Writing: Common Grammar, Usage, and Spelling Problems." August–September 2003. *http://www.io.com/~hcexres/tcm1603/acchtml/gramov.html.*

"Proofreading for Common Surface Errors." August–September 2003. *http://www.indiana.edu/~wts/wts/proofreading.html.*

"Purdue University Online Writing Lab (OWL)." 1995–2003. August–September 2003. *http://owl.english.purdue.edu.*

Grammar and Usage Resource Texts

Elbow, Peter. *Writing with Power: Techniques for Mastering the Writing Process.* New York: Oxford University Press, 1998

Elbow, Peter. *Writing Without Teachers.* New York: Oxford University Press, 1998.

Klauser, Henriette Anne. *Writing on Both Sides of the Brain.* San Francisco: Perennial Library, 1986.

Murray, Donald M. *The Craft of Revision.* New York: Heinle & Heinle, 2003.

Murray, Donald M. *Write to Learn.* New York: Heinle & Heinle, 2001.

Strunk, William Jr. and E.B. White. *The Elements of Style.* Boston: Pearson, Allyn, and Bacon, 2000.

Zinsser, William. *On Writing Well.* New York: HarperResource, 2001.

CAPT
Practice Tests

Writing Across The Disciplines

Writing Across the Disciplines contains three separate assessments:

- Two Interdisciplinary Writing Tasks
- One Editing and Revising Test

This portion of the book contains two complete practice tests for the CAPT task of Interdisciplinary Writing. Each test contains two controversial topics and three resource articles for each issue. Each topic is presented in a format that is similar to what you will find on the actual CAPT. Lined paper similar to the actual CAPT Answer Booklet is provided for each essay. A scoring rubric is included with each essay so that you can self-score and analyze your own writing.

- Read all the direction pages so that you become familiar with the test requirements.
- Write your essay using a Number 2 pencil.
- Have a highlighter on hand for marking important sections in the directions and in the articles.
- After you have read the directions, set a timer for 65 minutes, and then begin.

Practice Test 1—Interdisciplinary Writing Test

Issue One

Overview

The purpose of this interdisciplinary writing test is to determine how well you can write to persuade others to think as you do about an issue. In this test, you will read a few short articles about an important issue, take a position on the issue, and write a first draft of a persuasive letter. You must support your position with information from *each* of the source materials. Your response will be read and scored by trained readers.

About This Test

In this Interdisciplinary Writing test, you will think about and take a position on an important issue: **whether to remove the ban of cell phone use in school by students.** While you are working on this test, you will use skills and knowledge you learned in your language arts, mathematics, science, social studies, the arts, and other classes.

The Issue

In recent years, controversy has arisen over the ban on cell phone use in school by students. Because of present social trends toward increased use of cell phones by teenagers, some people believe that the time has come to remove the outdated ban on student use of cell phones in school. Those opposed to lifting the ban on student use of cell phones in school argue that such communication devices are simply a matter of convenience, not an issue of necessity.

WEEKLY READER   **FEBRUARY 22, 2002**

Calling Cell Phone Bans into Question

Is it time to put school cell phone bans on hold?

"Put them away! Put them away!" the school administrator yelled. A handful of students scrambled to stuff the contraband into their pockets and book bags. No, not drugs. Cell phones.

"I'm not in trouble, am I?" asked sophomore Neringa Eidimtaite, caught in the act of calling her dad for a ride home after finishing her midterm exams at Adlai E. Stevenson High School in Lincolnshire, Ill.

Neringa didn't get into trouble, but she had broken a new school rule on cell phones. Whereas Stevenson High used to ban cell phones completely from its school grounds, now Stevenson students are allowed to use their phones at school on weekends and after 3:25 p.m., the end of the school day. Neringa and the other students had made their calls at 11:15 a.m. because they had finished their midterms early and so were free to go home.

Times Have Changed

Situations like the one at Stevenson will likely have a familiar ring as more and more schools seek to lift bans and relax rules on cell phone use. Many schools adopted bans when cell phones were popular mainly with students who sold drugs. But times have changed, say many school administrators. Today, cell phones are commonplace. "Cellular communications are a part of living now," said Mike Stevens, principal of Prospect High School near Chicago, where restrictions were recently eased on cell phone use at school.

Some school districts have decided to change their policies because of the role cell phones have played in some emergency situations, such as the terrorist attacks of September 11, 2001, when victims used their cell phones to contact authorities and loved ones.

Emergency use is one reason Laura Rhodes, whose daughter Chris attends South Carroll High in Baltimore, Md., is glad the local school board is reconsidering its cell phone ban. "It makes you feel good," she said, "that your kid has an outside line if they need to get to you or to the police ...."

Hold the Phone

Still, some *schools* are holding the line, refusing to lift bans on the electronic devices. Cell *phones* won't ring anytime soon on campuses in Crosby, Texas, for example, said superintendent Don Hendrix. "The disruptions caused by cell phones would outweigh the advantages," Hendrix explained. "I don't buy the idea that you should [allow cell phones] because there's going to be a terrorist attack. That's silly."

Security expert Kenneth Trump said having hordes of students making emergency calls at the same time could actually hinder the sending of emergency messages by jamming phone lines.

You make the call: Should *schools* continue to ban cell *phones?* Why or why not?

SAN JOSE MERCURY NEWS   **FEBRUARY 25, 2002**

Four California Bills Would Ease Restrictions on Cell Phones at School

They've been banned in restaurants. Clicked off in galleries. Shunned in theaters. But cellular *phones* are enjoying huge, if covert, popularity on California school campuses.

Still, those indispensable gadgets—perfect for arranging a ride home from soccer practice or contacting family members in a crisis—are illegal on public school grounds.

At least for now.
Pushed by teens and school officials, four bills now working their way through the state legislature would ease 1980s restrictions on cell phones at schools. Those rules were aimed at keeping schools safe from drug deals. But since the Sept. 11 attacks and a string of school shootings, cell phones are viewed as security devices.

Despite the statewide ban, teens say colorful Nokias and sleek Star-Tacs are as ubiquitous as history books or wadded-up homework on campus. To escape detection, students stash phones in backpacks or secrete them in purses.

Willow Glen High School senior Rudy Cervantes guesses that half his classmates tote wireless phones to school—although most keep them hidden. Cervantes, 18, got a phone after he suffered a volleyball injury last year and couldn't reach his mom.

"I think it is a good idea to have them in case of emergency," he said. "But people who have them have to realize they shouldn't take advantage of them." At Logan High School in Union City, student leaders felt the 1988 law banning cellular phones, pagers and other "electronic signaling devices" was so retro that they proposed new legislation to state Sen. Liz Figueroa, D-Fremont. They will testify before lawmakers when the bill gets a committee hearing next month.

Safety Paramount
"When I think about cell phones, I don't think about drugs or gangs," said Logan senior Juan Pagan, a student representative to New Haven Unified's school board. "I think about safety, and calling your parents to get home." Figueroa contends it's important for the law to keep pace with technology.

"When this law was put into effect, they didn't know all of the ramifications and how the incredible use of cell phones would spread," she said. "Technology is changing, and it's necessary to catch up."

Her bill would allow individual districts to make rules so cell phones won't interfere with instruction. For instance, some schools could allow students to carry only phones that were off all day, while others might permit their use during lunch or breaks.

Assemblywoman Carol Liu, D-Pasadena, is sponsoring another bill, which already has passed the lower house 73–0. It would allow students to carry phones at school if they were turned off. Pupils could use phones to protect the "health and safety" of students, employees and visitors.

So far, there is no known opposition to ending the cell phone ban, Figueroa's staffers said. The state's school administrators group has not yet taken a stance on the matter, and the powerful California Teachers Association supports changing the law.

At schools around the Bay Area, principals and teachers say they're not worried that phones will be used to sell drugs. But some fear that the chirping gadgets could disrupt lessons and be a tempting target for theft, or that students might use them to play games instead of studying.

Many area schools say they do confiscate phones—and require a parent to retrieve them—if students are caught using them on campus. But they don't search backpacks or lockers for hidden phones.

On the other hand, at least two area schools—Palo Alto's Gunn High and Kennedy Middle School in Redwood City—allow students to bring cell phones or pagers to school with written permission from their parents.

Even if the law were changed, Kennedy Principal Warren Sedar said, "I would still want to see a parent permission slip because I'm concerned about them being stolen." Gunn's policy has been in place since the beginning of last school year. Principal Scott Laurence said he has 25 notes from parents explaining why their children need the wireless devices. Most of the notes say the children need phones to take care of younger siblings, keep in touch with parents who work far away or arrange rides home.

Gunn condones cell phones on campus as long as they are muted in classrooms and aren't disruptive when used outside.

That practice butts up against the law, but the Palo Alto Unified School District favors modernizing the Education Code to offer limited use of cell phones at school, an official said.

Changes Sought

"The law should be a living document," said Irv Rollins, an assistant superintendent in Palo Alto Unified. "What made sense back then doesn't make sense today." Like many safety measures, there's the potential for cellular phones to be abused at school, said Ronald D. Stephens, executive director of the nonprofit National School Safety Center in Westlake Village.

He supports ending the blanket ban, but says individual schools should make their own rules.

"The key here is distinguishing between appropriate and inappropriate uses and appropriate and inappropriate times," Stephens said.

David Bena said he urged his daughter, a freshman at Palo Alto High School, to bring a cell phone to school for safety and convenience.

"It's pretty obvious," said Bena, whose daughter Angelina calls home when she's ready to be picked up from water polo practice and theater rehearsals. "Disaster does happen at school. Cell phones are going to be the first communication if there's an emergency. The school office may not even know about it."

Source Three

CHICAGO TRIBUNE COMPANY   APRIL 17, 2002

Cell-Phone Freedom May Ring in Illinois Schools

Back in 1990, when Illinois lawmakers banned cell phones from public schools, it was hard to think of a reason a teenager might need one.

With their bulky bags and shrill electronic rings, the phones were an unwelcome classroom disruption. And they were so expensive, "the only kids who could afford cell phones were selling dope," said state Rep. Mary Flowers, (D-Chicago), who championed the ban.

Today, three out of four teens own cell phones, according to Teenage Research Unlimited, a market research firm based in Northbrook. Small enough to tuck in a backpack and virtually silent when set on "vibrate," the phones have become vital links between members of busy families. And with memories of Columbine, Sept. 11 and other disasters never quite at bay, the ability to connect instantly via the wireless telephones is a priceless reassurance.

"They are safeguards," said Flowers, who now is leading the charge to repeal the ban. "They are a parent's comfort zone."

Flowers, who failed last year to get the ban reversed, became even more determined after her frantic efforts to speak with her daughter at school Sept. 11. Despite repeated calls to the school office, Flowers couldn't get through.

"Had my daughter had a cell phone, she would have been able to call me," Flowers said.

Other parents recall the Columbine shootings three years ago, when students trapped inside the school were able to use their cell phones to call police and their parents.

"I just think it would be a good idea for my kids to have them available in case of such an emergency," said Theresa Heniff, a Tinley Park mother of two teenage daughters.

The current bill, which would leave it up to local school boards to either prohibit or regulate the use of cell phones by students, has passed the Illinois House overwhelmingly and now is before the Senate.

Not everyone thinks it's a good idea. In a poll of educators across the U.S. taken by the National Education Association last year, 76 percent said they were against students having cell phones or pagers in school.

But educators acknowledge that the ban is hard to enforce, and some even admit to looking the other way. Although students still bring the phones to school, they usually find it prudent to leave them turned off because a ringing phone is likely to be confiscated. Between classes, they use them to make calls from bathroom stalls or locker rooms.

"We found that a lot of students were already in possession of these cellular devices and were doing it in a clandestine manner that wasn't disruptive to education," said Prospect High School Principal Michael Stevens.

The school is in Arlington Heights High School District 214, which opted out of the cell phone ban shortly after Sept. 11. The law allows districts to exempt themselves if the school board and principals agree on rules for cell phone use on school property.

Jim Blaschek, student council president at Sandburg High School near Orland Park, has collected more than 1,000 signatures urging Consolidated School District 230 to opt out of the state ban. Blaschek wants cell phones available "for when we would really need them," such as an emergency in school or at home.

Most students want to carry the phones for convenience, so they can keep in touch with friends or family members.

Andrew Swanson, 18, a senior at Naperville Central High School, said he needs a phone to keep in contact with his mother, who is blind.

"I've got to drive her home [from work] because she can't see," he said. "If something happens and she left work early, I would know that I don't need to come and get her that day."

But not everyone favors lifting the ban. Some parents, especially those who can ill afford the cost of providing their children with cell phones, argue that there's no compelling reason for students to have them in school.

"If I need to reach my child in an emergency, I just go through the school office," said Judy McAllister of southwest suburban Homer Township.

Kenneth Trump, president of National School Safety and Security Services, a consulting firm based in Cleveland, said cell phones won't necessarily ensure greater safety in an emergency.

Hundreds of students trying to use their cell phones could jam lines or create confusion for emergency personnel, he said. Besides, he added, students looking for trouble find it easier to create an emergency, such as calling in a bomb threat, when they're allowed to carry cell phones.

"The argument that somehow students will be safer with cell phones in school in the aftermath of Columbine and Sept. 11 is bogus," Trump said. "The real reason why students and their parents want cell phones allowed on school property is simply a matter of convenience."

How to Write This Persuasive Essay

Writing the Introduction

Remember: A good introduction should:

- State the issue
- Show how it is controversial
- Show that you are an expert on the topic
- Take a stand
- Urge support

Reading the Directions

Before the start of this test, the teacher will read several pages of directions and ask you to follow along. This time is *not* part of your 65 minute test time. However, you can use this direction time to begin gathering information that you can later use in your persuasive letter.

The Issue

What Is the Issue?

In the actual Test Booklet on page 4, there is a section entitled "About this Test". In this paragraph you will find a sentence in bold print. As our teacher reads this section to you during the direction part of the test, use your **highlighter** to mark the bold print sentence that follows the phrase "take a position on an important issue:"

When you begin to write your letter, you can copy that sentence exactly into your introductory paragraph. This will prevent you from incorrectly stating the issue.

How Is It Controversial?

You will also find on page 4 of the actual Test Booklet, a section entitled "The Issue." As your teacher reads this paragraph to you during the directions, **highlight** the two sentences that show the controversial nature of the issue. The sentences always include the phrases "some people believe..." and "those opposed to the idea argue..." You can use these two sentences from the directions in your introduction to show your understanding of the topic.

To Whom Do I Write?

In the actual Test Booklet on page 5, there is a section entitled "Your Task". As your teacher reads this paragraph to you during the directions, look at the first bold print sentence. It says **"You will read a** few articles about..., take a position on the issue and write a persuasive letter to..." **Highlight** the person or group to whom you are to write your letter.

The Salutation

Begin your letter with "Dear," followed by the name of the person or group that you highlighted in the directions. For example, you can use *Dear Governor*, or *Dear Representative,* or *Dear Forest Service.*

Time

In the directions that your teacher will read to you during the test is a section entitled, "Organizing Your Time." It is suggested that you break up your 65 minutes into 2 parts: 30 minutes for reading and 35 minutes for writing your letter. Most students, however, choose not to follow that approach. Instead, it is far easier to begin writing your introduction immediately, decide your position on the issue, then read just enough information from each article to find material and quotes to support your position on the issue.

1. **Begin your introduction with the statement of the issue, exactly as it appears in the test directions section called** *"About this Test."*

   Some suggestions include:
   - The use of cell phones in school is a controversial issue across the country.
   - An issue that is often debated is the use of cell phones in school.
   - A topic that has received much attention recently is the proposal to lift the current ban on cell phone use in school.

2. **Show the reader how this issue is controversial.**

   To do this, use the two sentences that you highlighted in the section called "**The Issue.**" You may paraphrase the sentences in your own words, or use the wording in the test booklet.

   Some suggestions include:
   - Some people believe that the time has come to remove the outdated ban on student use of cell phones in school. Those opposed argue that such communication devices are simply a matter of convenience, not an issue of necessity.
   - Some people argue that the time has come to remove this outdated ban, while others suggest that student use of cell phones in school are merely for convenience, not necessity.
   - This debate over cell phone use in school by students is between those who believe it is time to end an outdated ban and those who view these devices as convenience, not necessity.

3. **Show that you are an expert on the topic of school cell phone bans.**

   To do this, write that you have read several articles on the topic.

   Some suggestions include:
   - I have read several articles on the topic of school cell phone use.
   - I have researched this topic.
   - I have investigated [explored, studied, looked into] the topic of cell phone use in school.

Finally, it is time to look at the three articles to decide which side of the issue you will support. Read the title of each article and any bold print headings. If there are no bold print headings in the article, read the first paragraph. This will usually give you a hint as to which side of the debate the article will present.

- The first article, "Calling Cell Phone Bans into Question," contains the heading, "Times Have Changed." So, you can assume this article probably favors ending the school ban on cell phones.
- The second article, "Four California Bills Would Ease Restrictions on Cell Phones at Schools," appears, just by its title, to probably contain some valid reasons to end the ban on school cell phones.
- The title of the third article, "Cell-Phone Freedom May Ring in Illinois Schools," also would tell you that it likely contains reasons why school cell phone bans are being lifted.

Therefore, although the three articles may give some reasons to continue the school cell phone ban, it appears that the best side to support in this essay is the side that favors ending the school cell phone ban.

4. State your position on the issue of school cell phone bans.

Since you know that ending the school cell phone ban will be the easiest side to defend in your letter, let the reader know that this is your position. You should say that you *strongly favor, believe,* or *support* an end to school cell phone bans.

5. Urge the reader to support your view and act on that support.

In this part of the introduction, use powerful words, such as "strongly encourage, or "highly recommend." For example, *I strongly encourage you to support an end to school cell phone bans.*

Reading the Articles

You will read the articles to find three reasons that you can use to support your stand on the issue of lifting school cell phone bans.

1. Begin reading the first article.

You are looking for a reason to lift the school cell phone ban. Look at the section under the heading "Times Have Changed." The second sentence is a good place to begin highlighting. Continue reading and highlighting through the next paragraph.

You now have a good first reason that you can use as information for your first body paragraph: *Times have changed since the original laws on cell phones in school were written.*

In the margin of the article, write *#1: times have changed.*

When you begin your letter you will refer back to this highlighted section. You do not have to spend time reading through the rest of this article, as you now have the information you need.

2. Begin reading the second article.

You are looking for a second reason to lift the school cell phone ban. Look at the fifth paragraph, which begins with "Pushed by teens and school officials …." Later in that paragraph is a sentence that states, "But since the September 11 attacks and a string of school shootings cell phones are seen as security devices." Highlight this sentence because it stresses the value of student access to cell phones during an emergency, and label it *#2: emergencies*. Also, the sentence that begins with "I think it is a good idea to have them in case of emergency …." should be highlighted and labeled *#2: emergencies*.

Additionally, highlight paragraph 11, which begins with "Assemblywoman Carol Liu …," because it gives the "health and safety of students" as another reason to lift the school cell phone ban. Label it, too, *#2: emergencies*.

Next look at paragraph 16, which begins, "Even if the law were changed …." The end of that paragraph states, "Most of the notes say that the children need the cell phones to take care of younger siblings, keep in touch with parents who work far away or arrange rides home." Highlight this sentence also and label it *#2: emergencies*.

These four ideas form a good second reason to favor the lifting of school cell phone bans: security and safety in times of school or family emergencies.

Also note that while you were reading short sections of this article, some information was given that would also support your first reason: *times are changing*. Highlight any of these and label them *#1*. For example, the paragraph that speaks of law as a "living document" and the sentence about "modernizing the Education Code" would both be good support for the fact that times have changed.

As you write your letter you will refer back to these highlighted sections. You do not have to spend time reading all through the rest of this article, as you now have the information you need.

3. Begin reading the third article.

You are looking for a third reason to lift the school cell phone ban. As you begin to read this article, notice that there are sections that support the first two reasons you have already selected to use. The third paragraph, which begins with "Today, three out four teens …," should be highlighted and labeled in the margin as *#1: changing times*. Paragraph 7, which begins with "Other parents recall the Columbine shootings …," should also be highlighted and labeled *#2* because it gives more support to your second reason: *emergencies*.

4. Find your third reason.

The third article briefly suggests a third reason that could be expanded using information from the first two articles: *cell phones in school are not a disruption.* Look at paragraph 11 and the sentence that begins with, "Although students still bring the phones to school ..." and the paragraph that follows it. Highlight these sections and in the margin, label them *#3: not a disruption.*

Do you remember reading anywhere in the other two articles where this idea was also mentioned?

In the second article, paragraph 10 discusses cell phone use that would not interfere with school instruction. This and the sentence that follows should be highlighted and labeled *#3: not a disruption.*

The first article also shows that the use of cell phones at school would not be disruptive. Read the second sentence in the third paragraph. "Whereas Stevenson High used to ban cell phones completely from its school grounds, now Stevenson students are allowed to use their phones at school on weekends and after 3:25 p.m., the end of the school day." It illustrates how cell phones can be used after school and on weekends without disrupting classroom learning. Highlight this section and in the margin, label it *#3: not a disruption.*

Writing the First Body Paragraph

A good body paragraph should:
- State a reason for your position
- Explain this reason
- Support it with a quote or reference to an article
- Further expand and explain the quote
- Restate your reason

1. State your first reason for opposing the ban on school cell phones.

Your first reason is that times have changed since the ban on cell phones first became law. Your opening sentence in the first body paragraph and in every body paragraph should contain your position and a reason: *One reason to lift the ban on school cell phones is that....*

2. Explain this reason.

Look back at the three articles for all the places that you marked a *#1.* Reread each of these labeled sections. Now, using that information, explain in your own words that cell phones are no longer a device just used by drug dealers and are now commonplace.

3. Support the first reason with a quote or reference from one of the articles.

You can choose from several good quotes to show that with changing times cell phones are commonplace and the laws should be changed:

- The statement by Mike Stevens of Prospect High School, found in the first article, in which he states, "Today, cell phones are commonplace. 'Cellular communications are a part of living now.'"
- The statement of Willow Glen High School senior Rudy Cervantes, found in the second article, in which he guesses, "...that half his classmates tote wireless phones to school..."
- The statement in the second article by Sen. Liz Figueroa. "Technology is changing, and it's necessary to catch up."
- The statement that three out of four teens own cell phones, found in the third article. It states, "Today, three out of four teens own cell phones, according to Teenage Research Unlimited..."
- The statement by Irv Rollins in the second article, in which he says, "The law should be a living document...What made sense back then doesn't make sense today."

Any of these would be a good reference to support your view that schools need to change with the times.

4. Expand on the idea expressed in the quote or reference.

In your own words, explain how cell phones are widely used and part of the new communication technology, and that school policies need to keep up.

5. Restate your first reason for opposing the ban on school cell phones.

This is the concluding sentence in your first body paragraph. It should be a statement of your view on the issue as well as a restatement of your first reason. For example, *Therefore, one reason to support ending the ban on school cell phone use is...*, or *Clearly, cell phones are now commonplace and the ban on them in school should be ended.*

As you practice writing body paragraphs, you will develop your own writing style and your favorite phrases for the concluding sentences of body paragraphs.

NOTE: After you have finished using information from an article, write "used" or put a check by the title of the article. This will help ensure that you use material from all three articles.

Writing the Second Body Paragraph

1. State your second reason for opposing the ban on school cell phones.

Always begin the second and third body paragraphs with a good transition sentence. Some suggestions include: *Another reason to lift the ban on school cell phones is...*, or *Lifting the cell phone ban is additionally important because...*

Your second reason to end the ban on school cell phones is that cell phones are essential for safety and emergencies.

2. Explain this reason.

Look back at the three articles and find where you marked a #2. Reread each of these labeled sections. Now, using that information explain in your own words that

- cell phones help families stay in touch during the day.
- students can contact parents for rides home.
- in times of emergency parents can be assured that their children are safe.

3. Support your second reason with a quote or reference from one of the articles.

There are several good quotes that you can choose from to show that cell phones are essential for communication among family members during family or school emergencies:

- The statement that students used cell phones to call police during the Columbine shootings, found in the third article. It states, "Other parents recall the Columbine shooting three years ago, when students trapped inside the school were able to use their cell phones to call police and their parents."
- The bill proposed by Assemblywoman Liu, found in the second article. In this bill, "Pupils could use cell phones to protect the 'health and safety' of students, employees and visitors."
- The statement by Laura Rhodes in the first article, in which she states, "It makes you feel good that your kid has an outside line if they need to get to you or to the police…"

Any of these would be a good reference to support your view that cell phones are essential in times of emergencies.

4. Expand on the idea expressed in the quote or reference.

In your own words, further explain how cell phones are essential for parents and students in times of family or school emergencies.

5. Restate your second reason for opposing the ban on school cell phones.

This is the concluding sentence in your second body paragraph. It should be a statement of your view on the issue as well as a restatement of your second reason. Such phrases as: *Therefore, another reason to support ending the ban on school cell phone use is…, or Clearly, cell phones are extremely helpful for security and in emergencies, so the ban on them in school should be ended.*

NOTE: After you have finished using information from an article, write "used" or put a check by the title of the article. This will help ensure that you use material from all three articles.

Writing the Third Body Paragraph

1. State your third reason for opposing the ban on school cell phones.

Always begin each body paragraph with a good transition sentence. Some suggestions include: *Another reason to lift the ban on school cell phones is...,* or *A third reason to...* or *Finally, lifting the cell phone ban is important because ....*

Your third reason to end the ban on school cell phones is that cell phones are not a disruption to the learning process in schools.

2. Explain this reason.

Look back at the three articles and find where you marked a *#3*. Reread each of these labeled sections. Now, using that information explain in your own words that

- cell phones can be kept on "silent mode" in school.
- students can use them only during lunch or after school.

3. Support your third reason with a quote or reference from one of the articles.

There are several good quotes that you can choose from to show that cell phones are not necessarily a disruption to the learning environment.

- The statement from the second article about Assemblywoman Liu's bill. The article states, "Her bill would allow individual districts to make rules so cell phones won't interfere with instruction."
- The statement about Gunn High School which says, "Gunn condones cell phones on campus as long as they are muted in classrooms and aren't disruptive when used outside."
- The statement by Rudy Cervantes, in the second article, where he refers to responsible use of cell phones. He states, "But people who have them have to realize they shouldn't take advantage of them."

Any of these would be a good reference to support your view that cell phones would not necessarily be disruptive in school.

4. Expand on the idea expressed in the quote or reference.

In your own words, further explain that cell phone use can be limited and can be silenced to prevent classroom disruptions.

5. Restate your third reason for opposing the ban on school cell phones.

This is the concluding sentence in your third body paragraph. It should be a restatement of your view on the issue as well as a restatement of your third reason. Such phrases as *Therefore, another reason to support ending the ban on school cell phone use is...,* or *Clearly, cell phones do not have to be a disruption so the ban on them in school should be ended.*

NOTE: After you have finished using information from an article, write "used" or put a check by the title of the article. This will help ensure that you use material from all three articles.

Writing the Conclusion

A good conclusion should:

- Restate your position on the issue
- List your reasons
- Urge support

1. Restate your position on the issue of lifting the ban on school cell phones.

You should state that after considerable research you believe that the ban on school cell phones should be lifted. For example: *Research therefore shows that the ban on school cell phones should be lifted.* Or, *the original ban on school cell phones should be lifted because the reasons used to prohibit cell phones are no longer valid.* Or, *banning school cell phones should therefore be removed.*

2. List your reasons for opposing the ban on school cell phone use.

In this sentence you should restate the three reasons you have relied on to support your view that cell phones should be allowed in school. For example, *Cell phones should be allowed in school because cell phones have become a part of everyday life, they are necessary for safety and emergency purposes, and they would not pose a disruption to classroom time.*

3. Urge support.

In this final sentence of the conclusion, you should ask the reader to agree with your position on the issue of cell phones in school and to act on that belief. For example, *I encourage you, therefore, to support the end to the ban on school cell phone use.* Or, *these reasons should convince you that the time has come to act and remove the ban on school cell phones.*

Self-Scoring Rubric

You can estimate what kind of score you will receive on an essay by using the self-scoring rubric below. Use this tool as you practice for the writing test. Look at each category. Circle the description in each category that best applies to your essay letter. You should have twelve circles when you have finished scoring your essay. Where do most of your scores fall? Three? Four? Five? Six?

Remember: Even if the rest of your eleven scores on these rubrics are fives and sixes, the scorers can rarely give you higher than a final score of four if you do not use all three sources.

Self-Scoring Rubric

	Categories	Three	Four	Five	Six
1	**Takes a stand**	yes, but not clearly developed	yes	yes	yes
2	**Persuasiveness**	not a very persuasive stand	somewhat persuasive	persuasive	very persuasive
3	**Awareness of audience**	some awareness	some awareness	awareness is evident	very aware
4	**Support**	some support	adequate support	well supported	richly supported
5	**Use of sources**	not all 3 sources used	not all 3 sources used	all 3 sources used	all 3 sources used
6	**Development of ideas**	few ideas are developed	adequately developed	well developed	very well developed
7	**Accuracy of information**	some inaccuracies/ irrelevant	some inaccuracies/ irrelevant	yes	yes
8	**Organization/ focus**	somewhat	adequate	well organized	very well organized
9	**Ideas**	not always clear	most ideas are clear	clearly expressed	clear and effective
10	**Flow of ideas**	choppy flow of thought	ideas and writing flow	generally flow	very fluent
11	**Transition**	lacking transitions	some transitions	good transitions	effective transitions
12	**Length**	less than 2 pages	2 pages	2½ pages	3 full pages

Practice Test 1—Interdisciplinary Writing Test

Issue Two

Overview

The purpose of this Interdisciplinary Writing Test is to determine how well you can write to persuade others to think as you do about an issue. In this test, you will read a few short articles about an important issue, take a position on the issue, and write a first draft of a persuasive letter. You must support your position with information from *each* of the source materials. Your response will be read and scored by trained readers.

About This Test

In this Interdisciplinary Writing Test, you will think about and take a position on an important issue: **whether the licensing of teenage drivers should be restricted.** While you are working on this test, you will use skills and knowledge you learned in your language arts, mathematics, science, social studies, the arts, and other classes.

The Issue

In recent years, controversy has arisen over the licensing of teenage drivers at age 16. Because of the dramatic increase in serious traffic accidents caused by teenagers, some people believe that raising the driving age will protect teenagers from the threat of their own driving risk. Those opposed to the idea of licensing restrictions for teenage drivers argue that teenagers are responsible drivers and should be given the opportunity to receive a driver's license at the age of 16.

Source One

THE ASSOCIATED PRESS

Bill Would Raise Driving Age to 17

When 16-year-old Jill Hurst got her driver's license, her mother was ecstatic.

Finally, there would be some relief. For years, Carrie Hurst had driven her daughter to dance practices, school, friends' houses. It's eight miles from their home in the tiny south Georgia community of Merriville to the nearest town, Thomasville.

"We don't even have a store," Carrie Hurst said. "It's just convenient for me" to have her daughter driving.

That's why she doesn't like the idea of raising the driving age in Georgia from 16 to 17, as one lawmaker has proposed.

"There is not that much more of a maturity level at 17," Carrie Hurst said. "If you were going to wait until they were mature enough, you'd have to wait until they're 21."

Supporters see the bill as a way to cut back on the number of accidents involving teens. Opponents argue it's a step that just isn't needed. Of particular concern are the differences between the heavily populated metropolitan areas and the less dense rural counties.

"In Atlanta, they've got buses, they've got taxis," House Speaker Tom Murphy said. "Out in rural Georgia, you don't have buses and most small towns don't even have taxis. How do kids get to work, how do they get to school?"

Freshman Sen. Phil Gingrey, R-Marietta, the bill's sponsor, said support seems to vary by geography more than political party. He said he understands opponents' concerns, but believes his bill will save lives in all parts of the state.

While teens in metro areas face heavy traffic, rural kids "have to worry about getting around logging trucks on curvy, winding roads," said Gingrey.

The bill, assigned to a Senate committee Thursday, has generated a lot of talk at the Capitol.

"It's not a bill that we're proposing, but over the years I have generally favored raising the driving age," Gov. Roy Barnes said. "This just says that the time for learners' permits is extended, and I think that's a good thing."

Sen. Steve Thompson, one of Barnes' floor leaders in the Senate, is a co-sponsor of the measure. Thompson, D-Powder Springs, is a former chairman of the Senate Transportation Committee.

Lt. Gov. Mark Taylor said the Senate seems divided over supporting Gingrey's bill or another expected bill that would require mandatory professional driving education.

With traffic growing every day, kids are scared to drive, said Sen. Michael Egan, R-Atlanta.

Just ask 16-year-old Daniel Huffsman of Marietta. If the driving age were raised, "I would give it up to be honest," said Huffsman, who limits his driving primarily to school and back. "I don't think people my age are ready to be driving. A lot of people I know are not the greatest drivers."

Egan said he supports the bill but would agree to different standards for different parts of the state if that could be done.

House Appropriations Chairman Terry Coleman, D-Eastman, said he doesn't think the bill is needed.

"For the most part, most teen drivers are safe," he said. "There may be a need for a more formal driver's education program. Parents have got to do something. I don't know that the government can do everything."

In addition to raising the driving age, Gingrey's bill would require teens to receive at least 50 hours of driving instruction, which could come from their parents.

Teenage drivers have already been a target of legislation in recent years. Stricter laws in 1997 gave the courts the authority to suspend the licenses of drivers younger than 21 for one serious infraction. State officials say crashes involving drivers ages 16–19 declined from 40,931 in 1997 to 38,382 in 1998.

Jill Hurst is just glad her 16th birthday came before any legislation raising the driving age could be passed.

"Our parents can't take us places and we don't have any other way to go," she said. Without the ability to drive, "I'd have to call a lot of people and find a ride."

Reprinted with permission of
The Associated Press.

TIME, INC.   1999

Too Young to Drive?

States are looking for a way to put the brakes on rising teen car accidents

When their high school let out at noon one Friday last month, Loren Wells and her four best friends embarked on two time-honored teenage traditions. First they went to the mall to shop for gowns for the junior prom this spring. Then they piled into Loren's black Chevrolet Corsica to go for a spin. At 3:45 that afternoon, a few miles from her home in Media, Pa., Loren's car began to drift off the highway, the sort of mistake seasoned drivers make—and correct—all the time. Sixteen-year-old Loren, who had got her license just 2½ months earlier, lurched back too far, lost control of the car and plowed into a tree with such force that everyone in the car was killed. The brand-new prom dresses did not go unworn. Three of the girls were buried in them.

For teens, there's no sweeter rite of passage than getting a driver's license. But an increasing number of them are driving to their deaths. While fatalities for most drivers have dropped in the past two decades, traffic deaths of newly licensed 16-year-olds surged about 50% between 1975 and 1996. Even more troubling than the rising body count are the reasons behind it. Alcohol, the main culprit in teen accidents in the '80s, is now much less of

a problem, thanks to a major educational blitz. Instead, safety specialists blame the sort of naïve errors that killed Wells and her friends. Citing cutbacks in driver education by schools, experts contend that young motorists simply have inadequate skills. Sean McLaurin, a highway-safety specialist for the National Highway Traffic Safety Administration, laments, "It's a silent epidemic."

A growing number of states are looking for a cure. After years of doling out licenses to 16-year-olds with a day's worth of classroom instruction and six hours of on-the-road practice, 24 states have passed graduated licensing laws that heavily restrict the youngest drivers. Similar proposals are pending in more than 15 other states. Though they vary in severity, these laws typically have three stages. First, at age 15 or 16, comes a learner's permit, with which the teen must clock up to 50 hours of adult-supervised driving. Then, about six months later, the teen can get a provisional license. Finally, the teen can get a full license, provided there have been no accidents or violations.

Some states, including California and Florida, have gone a step further, barring teens with provisional licenses from driving late at night, when the risk of accidents is higher. And six states have passed more radical laws prohibiting teens from driving with other teenagers in the car. "I've always believed that you put more than one teen in a car and their IQs go down," says Sandy Grasinger, who lobbied for the California law after her 15-year-old daughter died in an accident. "I did the same thing—radio going, hollering and talking and having fun."

It's too soon to tell whether the laws make for smarter drivers. But preliminary accident statistics in some states indicate they may be helping. In 1997, the first full year of graduated licensing in Florida, fatal and injury crashes among 15- to 17-year-olds fell 9%, according to the Insurance Institute for Highway Safety.

Still, there are doubters—and not just freewheeling teens. After years of playing chauffeur to so many sleepovers and swim practices, some parents find their own freedom limited by parental-supervision requirements. New Mexico Governor Gary Johnson has been vocal in his opposition to the graduated licensing bill making its way through that state's legislature. "[I] got my scooter license at 13," Johnson told the *Albuquerque Journal*. "I didn't want to be the guy that makes that harder for some

kids." Safety officials have another worry: passenger and curfew restrictions—like well-intentioned seat-belt laws—are almost impossible to enforce.

But advocates insist that just knowing they could get caught is enough to make teens more vigilant. The biggest deterrent may be the stories of kids like Loren Wells. That's why, besides pushing his state to adopt a stricter graduated licensing law, Pennsylvania Governor Tom Ridge is taking an extra precaution. "I cut out the articles about those girls," says Ridge. "And I've saved them to remind my own children down the road."

The New Road Rules
Tougher restrictions are spreading.

AGE: Teens must wait longer to hit the road; in six states they must be 18 to obtain a license without restrictions

CURFEW: 19 states bar *driving* late at night; North Carolina teens can't drive after 9 p.m. for the first six months

PASSENGERS: Six states limit them; California teens must wait six months to drive together

Source Three

THE CHRISTIAN SCIENCE MONITOR   1998

California Joins Movement to Restrict Teenage Driving
New graduated licensing system spreads, and will soon be in 22 states

For teenage drivers in a growing number of states, when Mom or Dad hand over the keys to the car, they're also more likely to be coming along for the ride.

California this week became the latest, and largest, addition to a movement making it tougher for teens to get full-fledged licenses. So-called graduated licensing systems, which include more parent time in the car, are in place or soon will be in 22 states. The goal is to reduce the death and accident rate for young adults on the roadways.

"We're close to the bandwagon effect," says Michael Smith, research psychologist with the National Highway Traffic Safety Administration (NHTSA), which wants a more restrictive system implemented in all states.

The lines were long at Department of Motor Vehicle offices throughout California as some young drivers sought to get driving permits the old-fashioned, easier way before July 1, when the new law took effect. But for the rest, the driving rite of passage will be more difficult than it was for their baby boomer parents, even though mobility seems more valued and necessary in the contemporary American household where both parents are increasingly apt to work.

But demographics and lifestyles give way to a grim statistic: Roadway accidents are the No. 1 cause of death for teens. While drivers under the age of 18 make up about 7 percent of the nation's driving population, they're involved in about 14 percent of the accidents. And though the number of teenage fatalities had been declining for a number of years due to higher drinking age limits, it has risen since 1992.

The core ingredients of California's new graduated licensing system:

- Lengthen the amount of time a new driver must hold a permit.
- Require that during the permit period an adult supervise the new driver for 50 hours on the road.
- Follow the permit with a provisional license that requires an adult in the car between midnight and 5 a.m. and whenever there are other passengers under age 20.
- Authorize a full license at 18 after a year of clean driving.

Despite the push by NHTSA, the American Automobile Association, and a number of other organizations, many states remain reluctant to implement the new system.

Iowa rewrote its law earlier this year but encountered some of the resistance that has surfaced in other states, particularly those with a tradition of early driving on the farm.

Iowa state Rep. David Heaton says advocates for changing the law in his state learned from the failures in Kansas and Tennessee. Iowa legislators worked closely with the state's Farm Bureau and other rural interests from the outset and were able to pass legislation in one session.

Iowa's system delays the age at which rural teens with special transportation needs get a license from 14 to 14½—and introduces a license for others that doesn't become a nonrestrictive license until the driver has a clean driving record for a year. The new law goes into effect Jan. 1, 1999. Other states implementing graduated licensing this year include Illinois, Louisiana, New Hampshire, and Ohio.

The higher accident rate of teens is attributable, in equal parts, to immaturity and inexperience, says Smith of NHTSA. The graduated system is an attempt to improve the early driving education with more adult supervision in the car. The slower progress to an outright license is also intended to increase the maturity and development of novice drivers.

Ezra Hauer, a transportation expert at the University of Toronto, says the question of when people are ready to drive, whether it's 14 or 18, is subjective. "You have to balance their need to drive as a means to socialize and see friends with the risks."

And while Hauer says tougher licensing requirements can reduce accident rates, their application in almost any age category would do the same.

How to Write This Persuasive Essay

Writing the Introduction

As you now know, a good introduction must:
- State the issue
- Show how it is controversial
- Show that you are an expert on the topic
- Take a stand
- Urge support

Reading the Directions

Before the start of this test, the teacher will read several pages of directions and ask you to follow along. This time is *not* part of your 65 minute test time. However, you can use this direction time to begin gathering information that you can later use in your persuasive letter.

The Issue

What Is the Issue?

In the actual Test Booklet on page 4, there is a section entitled "About this Test". In this paragraph you will find a sentence in bold print. As our teacher reads this section to you during the direction part of the test, use your **highlighter** to mark the bold print sentence that follows the phrase "take a position on an important issue:"

When you begin to write your letter, you can copy that sentence exactly into your introductory paragraph. This will prevent you from incorrectly stating the issue.

How Is It Controversial?

You will also find on page 4 of the actual Test Booklet, a section entitled "The Issue." As your teacher reads this paragraph to you during the directions, **highlight** the two sentences that show the controversial nature of the issue. The sentences always include the phrases "some people believe..." and "those opposed to the idea argue..." You can use these two sentences from the directions in your introduction to show your understanding of the topic.

To Whom Do I Write?

In the actual Test Booklet on page 5, there is a section entitled "Your Task". As your teacher reads this paragraph to you during the directions, look at the first bold print sentence. It says **"You will read a** few articles about..., take a position on the issue and write a persuasive letter to..." **Highlight** the person or group to whom you are to write your letter.

The Salutation

Begin your letter with "Dear," followed by the name of the person or group that you highlighted in the directions. For example, you can use *Dear Governor*, or *Dear Representative,* or *Dear Forest Service*.

Time

In the directions that your teacher will read to you during the test is a section entitled, "Organizing Your Time." It is suggested that you break up your 65 minutes into 2 parts: 30 minutes for reading and 35 minutes for writing your letter. Most students, however, choose not to follow that approach. Instead, it is far easier to begin writing your introduction immediately, decide your position on the issue, then read just enough information from each article to find material and quotes to support your position on the issue.

1. **Begin your introduction with the statement of the issue, exactly as it appears in the test directions section called "About This Test."**

    Some suggestions include:
    * Restricting teenage driving age is a controversial issue across the country.
    * An issue that is often debated today is the restricting of teenage driving.
    * A topic that has received much attention recently is the proposal to restrict teenage driving.

    In addition, when the issue involves a new law or changes to an existing one, it is a good idea to briefly explain the new law or the proposed changes. You might write: *Many states are raising the age at which teens can get full licenses while other states are proposing restrictions on the hours during which teens can drive.*

2. **Show the reader how this issue is controversial.**

    To do this, use the two sentences that you highlighted in the section called "The Issue." You may paraphrase the sentences in your own words, or use the wording in the test booklet.

    Some suggestions include:
    * Some people believe that raising the driving age will protect teenagers from the threat of their own driving risk. Those opposed argue that teenagers are responsible drivers and should be given the opportunity to receive a driver's license at the age of 16.

- The debate over the driving age is between those who believe restrictions will protect teenagers from their own driving risk and those who see teenagers as responsible and deserving the opportunity to receive a license at 16.
- Some people believe that teenagers will be protected from themselves if the driving age is raised, but others see teens as deserving the opportunity to get a license at 16.

3. Next, show that you are an expert on the topic of teenage driving.

To prove this, write that you have read several articles on the topic. Some suggestions include:

- I have read several articles on the topic of teenage driving licenses.
- I have researched this topic.
- I have investigated the issue of the licensing of teenage drivers.

Finally, it is time to look at the three articles to decide which side of the issue you will support.

This persuasive essay is not as simple to write as it appears! As a tenth grader this topic has special importance to you. Your first instinct may be to write an essay that favors keeping the issuance of driver's licenses at the present age, not raising the age nor placing more restrictions on teenage drivers.

Remember, however, that these articles are from newspapers which are regularly filled with stories of accidents involving teenagers. A quick look at the titles of the articles in this test will lead you to the conclusion that most of the information will probably favor raising the driving age and placing restrictions on teenage driving. You are, therefore, forced to write a persuasive letter to support a view that you, personally, probably disagree with.

It will be difficult to keep personal opinions and emotions from filling your letter. Remember, however, the scorers will be judging your letter on how well you used the source articles to write a strong persuasive letter.

Read the title of each article and any bold-print headings. If there are no bold print headings in the article, read the first paragraph. This will usually give you a hint as to which side of the debate the article will present.

- The first article, "Bill Would Raise Driving Age to 17," probably expresses the opinions of lawmakers who want to raise the driving age and place restrictions on teenage drivers.
- The second article, "Too Young to Drive?" appears, just by its title, to probably contain some valid reasons to raise the age and increase teenage driving restrictions.
- The title of the third article, "California Joins Movement to Restrict Teenage Driving," also would tell you that it likely contains reasons why the age for teenage driving should be raised.

Although the three articles may give some reasons to continue the present requirements for teenage drivers, it appears that the best side to support in this essay is the side that favors raising the driving age and placing more restrictions on teenage drivers.

4. State your position on the issue of restricting teenage driving.

Since you know that supporting these changes in the driving regulations will be the easiest side to defend in your letter, let the reader know that this is your position. You should say that you *strongly favor, believe,* or *support* restricting teenage driving.

5. Urge the reader to support your view and act on that support.

You might say: *"I strongly encourage you to support restrictions on teenage driving."*

Reading the Articles

You will read three articles to find three reasons that you can use to support your stand on the issue of raising the age for teenagers and imposing restrictions on teenage driving.

1. Begin reading the first article.

You are looking for a reason to raise the driving age and place more restrictions on teenage drivers. Paragraph 6, which begins "Supporters see the bill as a way …," is a good place to begin highlighting.

You now have a good first reason that you can use as information for your first body paragraph: *restricting teenage driving would reduce accidents.*

In the margin of the article, write *#1: reduce accidents.* When you begin your letter you will refer back to this highlighted section. You do not have to spend time reading all through the rest of this article, as you now have the information you need.

2. Begin reading the second article.

You are looking for a second reason to restrict teenage driving. Read the second paragraph. Highlight this paragraph because it gives good information and statistics that illustrate how restricting teenage driving would save lives. You now have a good second reason that you can use as information for your second body paragraph: *restricting teenage driving would save lives.*

In the margin of the article, write *#2: save lives.* Also highlight the last sentence of paragraph 4 and label it *#2* as well. This sentence reinforces the view that restricting teenage driving saves lives.

As you write your letter you will refer back to these highlighted sections. You do not have to spend time reading all through the rest of this article, as you now have the information you need to formulate a second reason.

3. Begin reading the third article.

You are looking for a third reason to restrict teenage driving. As you begin to read this article, notice that there are sections that support the first two reasons you have already selected to use. Paragraph 5 gives information to support the view that restricting teenage driving will save lives. Label that paragraph *#2: saves lives.*

This article briefly suggests a third reason that could be expanded using information from the first two articles: *teenagers are sometimes immature and inexperienced.*

Look at paragraph 11, which begins, "The higher accident rate ...." Highlight this paragraph and label it *#3: inexperienced and immature.* Do you remember reading anywhere in the other two articles where this idea was also mentioned?

The second paragraph of the second article should be highlighted and labeled *#3: inexperienced* because it mentions "naïve errors" and "inadequate skills." This second article also refers to the maturity level of teenage drivers. Read the second half of paragraph 4, which begins, "Some states ...." Highlight this section and in the margin label it *#3: immaturity.*

Writing the First Body Paragraph

A good body paragraph should:
- State a reason for your position
- Explain this reason
- Support it with a quote or reference to an article
- Further expand and explain the quote
- Restate your reason

1. State your first reason for favoring restrictions on teenage driving.

Your first reason is that accidents will be reduced. Your opening sentence in the first body paragraph and in every body paragraph should state your position and a reason. In this first paragraph, you might write, *One reason to restrict teenage driving is to save lives.*

2. Explain this reason.

Look back at the three articles and find all the places where you marked *#1: saves lives.* Reread each of these labeled sections. Now, using that information explain in your own words that:
- teenage drivers have a high fatality rate.
- statistics show this high fatality rate.

3. Support the first reason with a quote or reference from one of the articles.

There are several good quotes that you can choose from to show that restricting teenage driving will save lives:

- The statement about fatality rates, which is found in the first article states, "Supporters see the bill as a way to cut back on the number of accidents involving teens."
- The statement about the results in Florida, which is found in the second article, states, "In 1997, the first full year of graduated licensing in Florida, fatal and injury crashes among 15- to 17-year-olds fell 9%, according to the Insurance Institute for Highway Safety."
- The statement about roadway accidents, which is found in the third article, states, "Roadway accidents are the No. 1 cause of death for teens."

Any of these would be a good reference to support your view that restricting teenage driving saves lives.

4. Expand on the idea expressed in the quote or reference.

In your own words, further explain how restricting teenage driving will save lives.

5. Restate your first reason for favoring restrictions on teenage drivers.

This is the concluding sentence in your first body paragraph. It should be a statement of your view on the issue as well as a restatement of your first reason. You might use such phrases as: *Therefore, one reason to support increased restrictions on teenage driving is...,* or *Clearly, placing restrictions on teenage drivers will save lives.*

NOTE: After you have finished using information from an article, write "used" or put a check by the title of the article. This will help ensure that you use material from all three articles.

Writing the Second Body Paragraph

1. State your second reason for favoring restrictions on teenage driving.

Always begin the second and third body paragraphs with a good transition sentence. Some suggestions include: *Another reason to place restrictions on teenage driving is...,* or *Restricting teenage driving is additionally important because....*

Your second reason to restrict teenage driving is that it will *reduce accidents*.

2. Explain this reason.

Look back at the three articles and find the places where you marked a *#2*. Reread each of these labeled sections. Now, using that information explain in your own words that

- teenagers have higher accident rates than the rest of the population.
- the number of teenage accidents has decreased in states where these laws are in effect.

3. Support your second reason with a quote or reference from one of the articles.

There are several good quotes that you can choose from to show that restricting teenage driving will reduce accidents:

- The statement by Sen. Phil Gingery, in the first article, states that restrictions will save lives. He states that he…believes his bill will save lives...
- The statement about restricting night driving by teenagers in order to reduce teenage accidents is found in the second article. It states, "Some states, including California and Florida, have gone a step further, barring teens with provisional licenses from driving late at night, when the risk of accidents is higher."
- The statement in the third article about 14% of accidents states, While drivers under the age of 18 make up about 7 percent of the nation's driving population, they're involved in about 14 percent of the accidents.

Any of these would be a good reference to support your view that restricting teenage driving will reduce accidents.

4. Expand on the idea expressed in the quote or reference.

In your own words, further explain how restricting teenage driving will reduce accidents.

5. Restate your second reason for favoring restrictions on teenage driving.

This is the concluding sentence in your second body paragraph. It should be a statement of your view on the issue as well as a restatement of your second reason. You might write, *Therefore, another reason to support restrictions on teenage driving is…,* or *Clearly, restricting teenage driving will reduce roadway accidents.*

NOTE: After you have finished using information from an article, write "used" or put a check by the title of the article. This will help ensure that you use material from all three articles.

Writing the Third Body Paragraph

1. State your third reason for favoring restrictions on teenage driving.

Always begin the second and third body paragraphs with a good transition sentence.

Some suggestions include: *Another reason to place restrictions on teenage driving is…,* or *Restricting teenage driving is additionally important because….*

Your third reason to restrict teenage driving is that teenagers are often *immature and inexperienced drivers.*

2. Explain this reason.

Look back at the three articles and find the places where you marked a *#3*. Reread each of these labeled sections. Now, using that information explain in your own words that
- teenagers make errors that experienced drivers do not make.
- more practice is needed to gain experience.

3. Support your third reason with a quote or reference from one of the articles.

There are several good quotes that you can choose from to show teenagers often lack the maturity and experience needed to be safe drivers.
- The quote from Michael Smith about immaturity and inexperience, which is found in the third article, refers to this issue. It states, "The higher accident rate of teens is attributable, in equal parts, to immaturity and inexperience, says Smith of NHTSA."
- The statement by Sandy Grasinger in the second article refers to the maturity issue. It states, "And six states have passed more radical laws prohibiting teens from driving with other teenagers in the car. 'I've always believed that you put more than one teen in a car and their IQs go down,' says Sandy Grasinger, who lobbied for the California law…."
- The statement by Daniel Huffsman, from the first article, says "I don't think people my age are ready to be driving. A lot of people I know are not the greatest drivers."

Any of these would be a good reference to support your view that teenage drivers often lack maturity and experience.

4. Expand on the idea expressed in the quote or reference.

In your own words, further explain that teenagers need more experience and maturity to be safe drivers.

5. Restate your second reason for supporting restrictions on teenage driving.

This is the concluding sentence in your third body paragraph. It should be a restatement of your view on the issue as well as a restatement of your third reason. You might choose to use such phrases as, *Therefore, another reason to support restrictions on teenage driving is…,* or *Clearly, restrictions on teenage driving would promote more experience and maturity.*

NOTE: After you have finished using information from an article, write "used" or put a check by the title of the article. This will help ensure that you use material from all three articles.

Writing the Conclusion

A good conclusion should:
- Restate your position on the issue
- List your reasons
- Urge support

1. Restate your position on the issue of restricting teenage driving.

You should again state that after considerable research you believe that restrictions should be placed on teenage driving. For example, *Research therefore shows that restrictions should be placed on teenage driving.*

2. List your reasons for favoring restrictions on teenage driving.

In this sentence you should restate the three reasons you have relied on to support your view that teenage driving should be restricted. For example, *The laws regarding teenage driving should be made stricter because...,* or, *It is time to rewrite the driving laws for teenagers because....*

3. Urge support.

In this final sentence of the conclusion, you should ask the reader to agree with your position on the issue of restrictions on teenage driving and to act on that belief. For example, *In conclusion, I ask your support for laws that would place restrictions on teenage driving.* Or, *These reasons should convince you that the time has come to place restrictions on teenage driving.*

Self-Scoring Rubric

You can estimate what kind of score you will receive on an essay by using the following self-scoring rubric. Use this tool as you practice for the writing test. Look at each category. Circle the description in each category that best applies to your essay letter. You should have twelve circles when you have finished scoring your essay. Where do most of your scores fall? Three? Four? Five? Six?

Remember: Even if the rest of your eleven scores on these rubrics are fives and sixes, the scorers can give you no higher than a final score of four if you do not use all three sources.

Self-Scoring Rubric

	Categories	Three	Four	Five	Six
1	**Takes a stand**	yes, but not clearly developed	yes	yes	yes
2	**Persuasiveness**	not a very persuasive stand	somewhat persuasive	persuasive	very persuasive
3	**Awareness of audience**	some awareness	some awareness	awareness is evident	very aware
4	**Support**	some support	adequate support	well supported	richly supported
5	**Use of sources**	not all 3 sources used	not all 3 sources used	all 3 sources used	all 3 sources used
6	**Development of ideas**	few ideas are developed	adequately developed	well developed	very well developed
7	**Accuracy of information**	some inaccuracies/ irrelevant	some inaccuracies/ irrelevant	yes	yes
8	**Organization/ focus**	somewhat	adequate	well organized	very well organized
9	**Ideas**	not always clear	most ideas are clear	clearly expressed	clear and effective
10	**Flow of ideas**	choppy flow of thought	ideas and writing flow	generally flow	very fluent
11	**Transition**	lacking transitions	some transitions	good transitions	effective transitions
12	**Length**	less than 2 pages	2 pages	2½ pages	3 full pages

Practice Test One—Editing and Revising

In this test you are asked to edit and review examples of student writing. It measures your ability to use standard written English as well as to improve sentences. During this test you will read several passages and look for embedded errors and answer multiple choice questions to indicate appropriate corrections.

This test will focus on your knowledge and skills in the following specific areas.

Composing and Revising

A. ***Content, Organization, and Tone*** including topic sentence, supporting detail, extraneous material, logical order, tone and redundancy of ideas
B. ***Revision: Syntax*** including fragment, run-on; awkward construction, parallel construction and sentence combining
C. ***Revision: Word Choice*** including descriptive language, transition words, generality/specificity and misplaced modifiers

Editing

A. ***Capitalization*** including titles of people, proper nouns, proper adjectives, first word in dialogue and names of places, organizations, nationalities, buildings, historical events and works of art
B. ***Punctuation*** including the use of the comma, quotation marks, apostrophe, semicolon and colon
C. ***Usage*** including subject and verb agreement, verb tense, pronoun reference, pronoun case, indefinite pronoun, special problems in usage and adjective/adverb usage
D. ***Spelling***

In this test, the lines in each passage are numbered. This is to help you refer back to specific parts of the passage as you answer the questions. As you read each question, it is helpful to highlight the lines or words that are referred to in each question.

Remember the test has 3 passages, each with six questions and you are allowed 25 minutes for this test. Therefore, you should allow about 8 minutes for reading and answering the questions in each passage.

Each test in this section contains 3 passages, 18 questions on editing and revising as well as explanations of the correct answers.

Set your timer for 25 minutes and begin.

Test 1

Read the following articles and answer the multiple choice questions. You will have 25 minutes to complete this test.

Passage One

SUNWISE PROGRAM MEMO

A national agency has sent this memo to schools encouraging them to participate in a government program promoting safe exposure to sunlight. Read the memo and then answer the multiple-choice questions that follow.

1 Children spend lots of time outdoors during recess, physical education classes, after-
2 school activities, and sports programs. While some exposure to sunlight can be enjoyable
3 and healthy, too much can be dangerous. Children need to be physically active, but must
4 learn to protect themselves from overexposure to ultraviolet radiation. This overexposure
5 can cause serious health effects, including skin cancer and other skin disorders, eye
6 damage and cataracts, and immune system suppression. According to the American
7 Cancer Society, skin cancer is the most common type of cancer in the United States.
8 Children need sun protection education since unprotected exposure to the sun during
9 youth puts them at increased lifetime risk for skin cancer.
10 The SunWise School Program is an environmental and health education program that aim
11 to teach children and their caregivers how to protect themselves from overexposure to the
12 sun. Though the use of class, school, and community based components, SunWise seeks
13 to develop sustained sun-safe behaviors. The program encourages schools to provide a
14 sun-safe infrastructure, include shady areas and policies that promote sun protection.
15 Schools that register for the SunWise program will receive a kit containing lesson plans
16 and background information. The kit contains activities that combine education about
17 sun protection and the environment with other aspects of learning in a fun way. Being
18 apart of SunWise is a fun, easy, and effective way to protect the health of the children in
19 your school. The program focuses on the whole spectrum of health effects. Including
20 skin cancer, eye damage, and other illnesses.

Passage One Questions

1. What is the best change, if any, to make to the sentence in lines 2–3 (*While ... dangerous.*)?
    a. Change *dangerous* to **endangering.**
    b. Change *while* to **whilst.**
    c. Change the comma after *healthy* to a semicolon.
    d. Make no change.

2. What is the best change to make in the sentence in lines 10–12 (*The SunWise ... sun.*)?
    a. Change *environmental* to **environmentally.**
    b. Change *caregivers* to **caregiver's.**
    c. Change *protect* to **protecting.**
    d. Change *aim* to **aims.**

3. What is the best change to make in the sentence in lines 12–13 (*Though ... behaviors.*)?
    a. Insert a colon after *the use of.*
    b. Change *Though* to **Through.**
    c. Change *seeks* to **sought.**
    d. Change *behaviors* to **behaviours.**

4. Which of these revisions is the most effective for the sentence in lines 16–17 (*The kit ... way.*)?
    a. The kit contains fun activities that combine education about sun protection and the environment with other aspects of learning.
    b. The fun kit contains activities that combine education about sun protection and the environment with other aspects of learning.
    c. The kit of fun contains activities that combine education about sun protection and the environment with other aspects of learning.
    d. By having fun, students will learn about sun protection and the environment.

5. What is the best change, if any, to make to the sentence in lines 17–19 (*Being ... school.*)?
    a. Change *your* to **you're.**
    b. Change *effective* to **efective.**
    c. Change *apart* to **a part.**
    d. Make no change.

6. What is the best way to change the sentence fragment in lines 19–20 (*Including ... illnesses.*)?

a. The program focuses on the whole spectrum of health effects, including skin cancer, eye damage, and other illnesses.

b. The program focuses on the whole spectrum of health effects, in which are included the following: skin cancer, eye damage, and other illnesses.

c. The program focuses on the whole spectrum of health effects, skin cancer, eye damage, and other illnesses.

d. The program foci including health effects like skin cancer, eye damage, and other illness.

Passage Two

EXPERT PANELS

Elaine has written this essay for her civics class. Read the essay, then answer the multiple-choice questions that follow.

1   The use of court-appointed experts is an extraordinary technique that is appropriate when
2 the evidence is especially demanding and the opportunity for reasoned and principled
3 consideration based on submissions by the parties has been exhausted or offers little
4 promise. The difficulty of accomodating the conflicting values of science and law within
5 such a process is unlikely to satisfy those who insist on the deliberate and open-ended
6 consideration that is characteristic of science, or those who insist on the speedy and
7 certain resolution of issues that is valued by law. In the best of circumstances, such
8 appointments are regarded as a procedure that should be invoked only after careful
9 thought.
10   Despite the high quality of information developed by the expert panels, interviews with
11 participants in two programs revealed a number of difficulties that are likely to arise
12 again if such panels are developed for future litigation. Here are some suggestions for
13 judges to consider when appointing and using such panels. Most of these were explicit
14 comments from the participants or implicit in the comments of multiple participants.
15   The court should fully explore the opportunity to develop the information necessary for
16 thoughtful consideration of complex evidence without taking the extraordinary step of
17 appointing one or more experts. Even in the best of circumstances, such appointments of
18 panels of experts are costly and time consuming, present difficult issues of
19 administration, and raise concerns about the independence of judicial consideration.
20   Lots of thought should be given to the role that the appointed experts will play in the
21 litigation. The anticipated role of the experts will determine the legal authority that the
22 court invokes to undertake the appointments. At the beginning of the process, the court
23 should generally articulate the questions it wants the technical advisors or court-
24 appointed experts to address. Doing so will help define whether technical advisors or court-
25 appointed experts are needed, who they ought to be, what they should be asked to
26 do, and how they should present their conclusions.

Passage Two Questions

1. What is the best change to make, if any, to the sentence in lines 4–7 (*The difficulty ... law.*)?
   a. Change *difficulty* to **difficulties.**
   b. Change *those* to **these.**
   c. Change *accomodating* to **accommodating.**
   d. Make no change.

2. What is the best change to make, if any, to the sentence in lines 7–9 (*In the ... thought.*)?
   a. Insert a comma after *appointments.*
   b. Change a *procedure* to **procedural.**
   c. Change *invoked* to **invoking.**
   d. Make no change.

3. What is the best change to make in the sentence in lines 10–12 (*Despite ... litigation.*)?
   a. Change *expert* to **experts.**
   b. Change *participants* to **participant's.**
   c. Delete the word *again.*
   d. Change *litigation* to **litigiousness.**

4. What is the best change to make, if any, to the sentence in lines 17–19 (*Even ... consideration.*)?
   a. Change *panels of experts* to **expert panels.**
   b. Change *panels of experts* to **panels of experienced people.**
   c. Change *panels of experts* to **panel's of experts.**
   d. Make no change.

5. Which of these revisions is the most effective for the sentence in lines 20–21 (*Lots ... litigation.*)?
   a. People should think about the job that appointed experts will play in the litigation.
   b. Careful consideration should be given to the role that the appointed experts will play in the litigation.
   c. Carefully consider the role that appointed experts will play in the litigation.
   d. Appointed experts will need to give careful thought to the role they will play in the litigation.

6. What is the best way to change the sentence in lines 22–23 (*At the … address.*)?

    a. Delete *generally.*

    b. Change *wants* to **wanted.**

    c. Insert a comma after *beginning.*

    d. Change *articulate* to **articulating.**

Passage Three

FINANCE AND LEGISLATION OF RAIL

Laurel has written this essay for her history class. Read the essay, then answer the multiple-choice questions that follow.

1   Federal assistance to railroads began, as the industry sought to expand westward.
2   Starting in 1850, land grants were made to railroads as they attempted to reach the
3   Pacific. Federal regulatory power, however, was not established until 1887, when the
4   Interstate Commerce Commission (ICC) was created and given authority to set some rail
5   rates. Between 1893 and 1921, Congress passed several rail safety acts and gave ICC
6   responsibility for implamenting and enforcing the regulations. Little important railroad
7   legislation was passed during the next 40 years, and railroad dominance in transportation
8   declined, as Federal aid spurred expansion of the highway system and growth in the
9   trucking industry.
10   Starting in 1965, legislation gradually transferred all safety responsibility from ICC to
11   the Department of Transportation, including responsibility for regulations, inspection,
12   enforcement, accident investigation and recordkeeping, and some hazardous materials
13   functions. Railroads have played an important role in transportation. However, ICC
14   retained authority for railroad accounting and costing procedures, construction and
15   abandonment of rail lines, mergers, acquisitions, and issuance of securities. ICC also
16   enforced the "common carrier obligation," which requires a carrier to provide service to
17   anyone who seeks it and is willing to pay the charge published on rate schedules.
18   ICC requirements constrain railroads' abilities to compete economically with trucks and
19   played a crucial role in declining rail economic performance. By the early 1970s, seven
20   railroads that had provided freight and passenger service in the Northeast and Midwest
21   were bankrupt. From their remnants, federal action created the Consolidated Rail
22   Corporation (Conrail). A private freight railroad company with government financing
23   and oversight. At the same time, the quasi-public National Rail Corporation (Amtrak)
24   was created to provide passenger service.

Passage Three Questions

1. What is the best change, if any, to make in the sentence in line 1 (*Federal ... westward.*)?
   a. Delete the comma after *began.*
   b. Change *sought* to **sot.**
   c. Change *railroads* to **railroads'.**
   d. Make no change.

2. What is the best change, if any, to make in lines 5–6 (*Between ... regulations.*)?
   a. Change *gave* to **give.**
   b. Change *implament* to **implement.**
   c. Change *enforcing* to **enforced.**
   d. Make no change.

3. The sentence that does not belong in this passage is the sentence in
   a. line 2–3 (*Starting ... Pacific.*).
   b. line 13 (*Railroads ... transportation.*).
   c. lines 15–17 (*ICC ... schedules.*).
   d. lines 23–24 (*At ... service.*).

4. What is the best change to make to the sentence in lines 18–19 (*ICC ... performance.*)?
   a. Change *constrain* to **constrained.**
   b. Insert a comma after *economically.*
   c. Change *declining* to **declaring.**
   d. Change *rail* to **rail's.**

5. What is the best way to change the sentence fragment in lines 22–23 (*A private ... oversight.*)?
   a. From their remnants, federal action created the Consolidated Rail Corporation (Conrail), a private freight railroad company with government financing and oversight.
   b. From their remnants, federal action created the Consolidated Rail Corporation (Conrail): a private freight railroad company with government financing and oversight.
   c. From their remnants federal action created the Consolidated Rail Corporation (Conrail) a private freight railroad company with government financing and oversight and a private passenger service called Amtrak.
   d. From their remnants, federal action created the Consolidated Rail Corporation (Conrail), and a private freight railroad company with government financing and oversight.

6. What is the best change, if any, to make in the sentence in lines 23–24 (*At ... service.*)?

    a. The psuedo-public National Rail Corporation (Amtrak) was created at the same time to provide passenger service.

    b. The simultaneous quasi-public National Rail Corporation (Amtrak) was created at the same time to provide passenger service.

    c. Creating at the same time, a simultaneous quasi-public National Rail Corporation.

    d. Make no change.

Answers and Explanations

Passage One

1. **d.** The sentence does not need editing.
2. **d.** The subject of the sentence is singular, so the verb must also be in the singular form.
3. **b.** Although *though* is a word, this is most likely a typo. The word *through* makes more sense in this context.
4. **a.** The word *fun* modifies *activities*.
5. **c.** *Apart* means to be separate from. To be *a part* of something means to belong.
6. **a.** Choice b is too wordy. Choice c is a run-on sentence. Choice d is still a fragment.

Passage Two

1. **c.** *Accommodating* is the correct spelling.
2. **d.** The sentence is correct as written.
3. **c.** The word *again* is redundant.
4. **a.** *Expert panels* is succinct and accurate.
5. **b.** The language in choice a is too casual. Choice c has a shift in address by making *careful* into an adverb. Choice d changes the subject of the sentence, and therefore changes the sentence's meaning.
6. **a.** The word *generally* makes this sentence wordy.

Passage Three

1. **a.** The comma in the sentence is unnecessary.
2. **b.** *Implement* is the correct spelling.
3. **b.** This sentence is out of place.
4. **a.** The word *constrained* agrees in tense with the rest of the sentence.
5. **a.** Choice b does not use the colon correctly. Choice c is a run-on sentence. Choice d changes the meaning of the original sentence.
6. **d.** The original sentence is correct.

Practice Test Two

Issue One

Overview

The purpose of this interdisciplinary writing test is to determine how well you can write to persuade others to think as you do about an issue. In this test, you will read a few short articles about an important issue, take a position on the issue and write a first draft of a persuasive letter. You must support your position with information from *each* of the source materials. Your response will be read and scored by trained readers.

About this Test

In this Interdisciplinary Writing test, you will think about and take a position on an important issue: **whether students should be required to pay in order to participate in school athletic teams.** While you are working on this test, you will use skills and knowledge you learned in your language arts, mathematics, science, social studies, the arts, and other classes.

The Issue

In recent years, controversy has arisen over requiring student athletes to pay in order to play high schools sports. Because of the rapidly expanding costs of high school athletic programs combined with school budget deficits, some people believe that student athletes should pay to play high school sports. Those opposed to the idea of pay-to-play argue that athletic programs are a major part of high school and students should not have to pay in order to participate.

Article One

LANSING STATE JOURNAL   **MARCH 11, 2003**

Pay to Play: Sports Fees Inevitable, but No Student Should Be Denied

You can't get within a mile of a government or school budget without hearing someone say, "Unfortunate, but necessary."

The phrase applies to all the usual suspects—program cuts, service reductions, potential layoffs ... and, more than ever, charging students to play high school sports.

East Lansing, Okemos, Haslett and Webberville are among area schools either considering a charge, or raising existing fees.

East Lansing may charge $250 per sport per student, making it one of the highest pay-to-play school districts in Michigan.

Sad to say, such measures ARE unfortunate, but necessary. East Lansing schools must grapple with an estimated $4.2 million budget shortfall in the coming school year. It's part of an increasingly gloomy picture for Michigan's public schools, which took a $127 million hit overall during an emergency state budget cut this year.

Far better to charge student athletes, if it will help save some academic program or school service—or simply help balance the district's budget.

Yet schools, and the communities they serve, must not be too coldly calculating as they finagle the bottom line.

All should operate from the premise that no student should be denied a chance to play sports because his or her family can't afford it.

True, most if not all schools have some sort of scholarship mechanism to help needy families whose children want to play sports. But raising participation fees could strain more family budgets, especially those families with several students eyeing high school sports.

Here is where the Michigan High School Athletic Association can play a vital role. The MHSAA is working on a guide to sports participation fees. That's good.

But the association could also be a conduit for sharing ideas on how different Michigan communities handle pay-to-play fees.

Communities that rely on fund-raisers to help defray athletic fees will need to be more creative and more diligent to cover rising costs.

Businesses should be contacted about their willingness to sponsor several pay-to-play scholarships. Eligible students should be given chances to pay for their sports fees through community work or business partnerships.

While not integral to academics, athletics help students with everything from self-esteem to discipline. It's within that framework that communities opting

for pay to play must promise all students they won't be denied based on their families' income.

Reprinted with permission of
Lansing State Journal, March 11, 2003.

Article Two

NORWICH BULLETIN   **JUNE 18, 2002**

Plainfield Students Will Pay to Play
School Budget Cutbacks

BY MICHAEL LEMANSKI

At 17, Plainfield High School junior class president Kim Bettencourt says this should be the most memorable time of her life.

But next year, while planning for college, Bettencourt will do something no eastern Connecticut public high school student likely has done before: pay to participate in sports or her favorite club.

"Parents can't afford it," Bettencourt, who hopes to run track and play softball, said. "High school is supposed to be the [most enjoyable] time of our lives and we have to deal with stupid budget things."

The Board of Education Monday created a "student activity fee," a revenue-generating proposal some hope will stave off future budget cuts.

Next year, Plainfield High School students will pay a one-time, $50 fee to play sports or participate in clubs. Younger students in the elementary schools and middle school will pay $25.

This may be the first such policy in eastern Connecticut, as towns struggle to balance existing programs and budget cuts.

According to a 2000 Connecticut Interscholastic Athletic Conference study, 13 of 125 public high schools responding have "pay-to-play" systems in place—a little more than 10 percent.

But of those schools, none is in Windham or New London counties. In fact, most towns with such systems tend to be wealthier communities.

"It's beyond just sports," school board Vice Chairman Michael Saad said. "You pay that thing and you can do what you want to."

School officials say revenue issues fueled the move, adding the alternative is elimination of programs and, possibly, teaching positions.

Plainfield is trying, for a third time, to pass a budget for 2002–03. So far, the school system will lay off 23 certified staff, mostly teachers, as part of its $25 million school budget. The budget next goes to a vote June 24.

What could go next is why student activity fees are happening. "We're bound to generate revenues in one fashion or another," high school Principal Charles Langevin explained. "It's either do it this way or eliminate more teaching positions."

A Trend

State Department of Education spokesman Tom Murphy said "pay-to-play" or "pay-to-participate" options often are a last resort for cash-strapped school districts to avoid cuts in activities.

Murphy said, often, the "pay-to-play" scenario is temporary, as communities rally the next year and affected groups are reinstated to full funding.

But in other cases, the town becomes revenue dependent and it's up to the participants to fund sports and clubs.

Murphy said towns often make scholarships available for those who are not able to pay. Plainfield has not established a policy yet but has said it will not leave anyone out.

RHAM High School, which serves the towns of Hebron, Andover and Marlborough, is locked in its own budget battle this year, with "pay-to-play" on the table. Such a policy has been mentioned in Killingly, too.

According to RHAM Athletic Director Ed Bobinsky, the issue is simple: as a public high school, it's up to the school system to fund such activities. "Students shouldn't have to pay to play," Bobinsky said Monday. "That's the way I feel about it."

Last year, Regional School District No. 8—RHAM's regional school district—studied schools in the state that have such programs. Part of its data was the CIAC report.

What the RHAM study showed is towns with "pay-to-play" are not poor.

Simsbury, for example, charges $75 per student per sport, a staggering figure compared to Plainfield's proposed, one-time $50 fee for all activities in a year.

If a three-sport student-athlete wants to play in Simsbury, it costs $225.

Simsbury does have a $300 cap per sport per family, so if the starting five on the basketball team are all brothers or sisters, that family pays only $300, not $375.

Simsbury High Principal Dennis Carrithers said "pay-to-play" is accepted in the affluent Hartford suburb.

"A lot of families were OK with paying it, because they would rather have the chance for the activities continuing versus losing it," Carrithers said, adding Simsbury's fee was a product of budget problems 10 years ago.

Carrithers said, out of Simsbury's $45 million budget, student sport fees have meant $113,000 in revenue.

Tough for Plainfield
But Simsbury's per capita income—according to the state—is $44,617, more than double Plainfield's per capita income of $20,721.

That disparity was not lost on student leaders.

"I can definitely tell you that not as many people would be involved if they have to pay," senior class president Amy Bogert said. "I hope that doesn't happen."

In addition to students and families not having the extra money, she said such a proposal may backfire, as students would avoid clubs or sports.

After all, Bogert said, why would a student try out for a club they're not sure of if it could cost them money?

"I think all sports and clubs will see a dramatic decrease in players," Bogert said. "We have a hard enough time trying to get people involved."

School officials say the initial foray is not expected to have a huge monetary impact. Rather, they say, it is to see how much revenue it could generate should this be an issue in the future.

In addition, public service-oriented groups—such as SADD, the National Honor Society and Student Council—would not be impacted. It would apply mostly to clubs and sports.

"Once we see how it works, it could, potentially, increase to $100 or $200 next year," Board of Education Chairwoman Virginia Sampietro said.

In fact, school officials estimate about 100 high school students probably would have to pay the fee next year—which would raise only $5,000, Sampietro said.

As a result, the estimated revenue is not being included as part of a recent $450,000 budget cut package approved Monday.

"We just have no history, so we don't want to budget and not be able to collect several thousand dollars," Sampietro said.

Reprinted with permission of
Norwich Bulletin, Norwich, CT.

Article Three

THE CHRISTIAN SCIENCE MONITOR   SEPTEMBER 20, 2002

Will Pay-to-Play Ruin School Sports?

BY JUSTIN BROWN

As sports teams begin practice this year at schools across the country, many parents and student athletes are realizing that it may take more than just talent to make the cut.

Increasingly, schools are charging participation fees to be on a team—a trend that educators and sports advocates say is the concept of public education and the overall effort to get more kids involved in athletic activities.

"Pay-to-play" programs, as they are called, generally charge students about $50 to $250 per season.

Sometimes the fees are greater. In Worcester, Mass., for example, Oakmont Regional High School charges student athletes more than $1,000 to play football.

Although some schools give exceptions for athletes who cannot afford the fee, parents and administrators have raised concern about creating a two-tier system at a public school, in which some kids have to pay, and others don't. Moreover, it would be awkward, at the very least, for a student to have to claim financial hardship to a coach or athletic department.

"It's a big issue here," says Gayle Mulligan, a mother of two who was involved in protesting a pay-to-play proposal in Hebron, Conn. "Hebron is traditionally a farming town. [Participation fees] would be unfair for families who could not afford them. It could make a big difference for some kids when they decide if they want to go out for a team."

Moreover, observers say, the implementation of pay-to-play seems to lead to lower participation—at a time when participation is rising in schools that don't charge to play sports. The implication, should the trend continue, is that playing a sport at a public high school is a privilege to be paid for, not something earned through effort.

"Our position is that we oppose it philosophically," says Tony Mosa, the director of the Connecticut Interscholastic Athletic Conference. "Our athletic directors oppose it, and our coaches oppose it.

"We have found that there is some drop-off in participation when pay-to-play is implemented. We have also found that, in some instances, parents feel that because they are paying they have the right to control when their child plays in a game.

There are some aggressive parents out there, and this is causing problems."

Nationally, pay-to-play programs are clearly on the rise, although there are no hard statistics from the National Federation of State High School Associations (NFHS). The evidence is anecdotal.

A recent poll in Wisconsin found that 269 out of 493 schools were charging participation fees. Many of the schools with pay-to-play are in urban areas, says Todd Clark, a spokesman for the Wisconsin Interscholastic Athletic Association.

This year Carroll County, Md., became the first school system near Baltimore to implement sports fees. In Strongsville, Ohio, students will have to pony up $120 per sport—with a cap of $240 for a multisport athlete. At Overlook Middle School near Worcester, Mass., soccer now costs $342 and field hockey $389.

Meanwhile, some schools that already charged fees are upping the ante this year. In Minnesota, five high schools in the Anoka-Hennepin area raised fees by $80 per sport, bringing the charge for football to $290 and basketball to $332.

"My sense is that participation fees are increasing throughout the country," says John Gillis, assistant director of the NFHS, who began following the issue when it surfaced some 10 years ago.

According to Gillis, there are more than just economic reasons to explain the rise of pay-to-play programs. He points to cultural changes that have taken place over the past 20 to 30 years, in which the local

high school and its sports team are no longer the focus of small communities, as they once were.

As a result, athletic programs receive a smaller portion of school budgets than they once did—now about 2 to 3 percent. At the same time, they are becoming more expensive to run than ever before.

Also, Gillis says, with more activities available to the public, fewer fans are going to sporting events at the local high school. That has cut income from ticket sales.

Under the gun, athletic directors have had to resort to creative methods to find funds. One answer: pay-to-play.

"I can understand the controversy," NFHS's Gillis says. "Here you have a public school that the parents are paying taxes to support. Why should the parents have to pay extra for something that should be included with the school?"

In most instances, schools justify participation fees as necessary for survival.

Connecticut is typical of a state in which participations fees are becoming more common. With the economy in recession, the state has cut funding for schools. At the same time, the legislature has passed laws to increase standardized testing and to boost resources for special education—two expensive undertakings. Add it all up, and something has to give.

Often the local board of education will tell a school there is not enough money to fund a particular sports program. The school is then left with a choice: Cut the sport or look for other sources of money.

"We're against the concept of pay-for-play. We think the problems far outweigh the benefits," says Ed Goldstone, principal of Amity Regional High School in Connecticut. "We are an affluent district, but that does not mean that every family is affluent. If you have a sport like cross-country, where there are 40 kids participating and [even if] only five of them are affected, well, that's inexcusable."

Reprinted with permission of Justin Brown.

How to Write This Persuasive Essay

Writing the Introduction

As you now know, a good introduction must:
- State the issue
- Show how it is controversial
- Show that you are an expert on the topic
- Take a stand
- Urge support

Reading the Directions

Before the start of this test, the teacher will read several pages of directions and ask you to follow along. This time is *not* part of your 65 minute test time. However, you can use this direction time to begin gathering information that you can later use in your persuasive letter.

The Issue

What Is the Issue?

In the actual Test Booklet on page 4, there is a section entitled "About this Test". In this paragraph you will find a sentence in bold print. As our teacher reads this section to you during the direction part of the test, use your **highlighter** to mark the bold print sentence that follows the phrase "take a position on an important issue:"

When you begin to write your letter, you can copy that sentence exactly into your introductory paragraph. This will prevent you from incorrectly stating the issue.

How Is It Controversial?

You will also find on page 4 of the actual Test Booklet, a section entitled "The Issue." As your teacher reads this paragraph to you during the directions, **highlight** the two sentences that show the controversial nature of the issue. The sentences always include the phrases "some people believe..." and "those opposed to the idea argue..." You can use these two sentences from the directions in your introduction to show your understanding of the topic.

To Whom Do I Write?

In the actual Test Booklet on page 5, there is a section entitled "Your Task". As your teacher reads this paragraph to you during the directions, look at the first bold print sentence. It says **"You will read a** few articles about..., take a position on the issue and write a persuasive letter to..." **Highlight** the person or group to whom you are to write your letter.

The Salutation

Begin your letter with "Dear," followed by the name of the person or group that you highlighted in the directions. For example, you can use *Dear Governor*, or *Dear Representative,* or *Dear Forest Service.*

Time

In the directions that your teacher will read to you during the test is a section entitled, "Organizing Your Time." It is suggested that you break up your 65 minutes into 2 parts: 30 minutes for reading and 35 minutes for writing your letter. Most students, however, choose not to follow that approach. Instead, it is far easier to begin writing your introduction immediately, decide your position on the issue, then read just enough information from each article to find material and quotes to support your position on the issue.

1. **Begin your introduction with the statement of the issue, exactly as it appears in the test directions section called *"About This Test."***

   Some suggestions include:
   - Pay-to-play high school sports is a controversial issue across the country.
   - An issue that is often debated today is the policy of high school students paying to play high school sports.
   - A topic that has received much attention recently is the proposal to require students to pay-to-play high school sports.

   In addition, since this issue involves a new policy, it is a good idea to briefly explain the new law or the proposed changes. You might write: *Many states are now charging fees to students in order to belong to a high school sports team.*

2. **Show the reader how this issue is controversial.**

   To do this, use the two sentences that you highlighted in the section called "The Issue." You may paraphrase the sentences in your own words, or use the wording in the test booklet.

   Some suggestions include:
   - Some people believe that student athletes should pay to play high school sports. Those opposed to the idea of pay-to-play argue that athletic programs are a major part of high school and students should not have to pay in order to participate.
   - The debate over pay-to-play is between those who believe athletes should share the cost of sports programs and those who argue that sports are a part of high school and students should not have to pay to participate.
   - Those who favor pay-to-play argue that students should pay to cover the cost of athletic programs, while those opposed believe that participation in sports is a regular part of high school.

3. Show that you are an expert on the topic of pay-to-play.

Write that you have read several articles on the topic. For example:

- I have read several articles on the topic of pay-to-play high school sports.
- I have researched this topic.
- I have investigated the issue of pay-to-play high school sports.

Finally, it is time to look at the three articles to decide which side of the issue you will support.

Read the title of each article and any bold-print headings. If there are no bold-print headings in the article, read the first paragraph. This will usually give you a hint as to which side of the debate the article will present.

- The first article, "Pay to Play: Sports Fees Inevitable, but No Student Should Be Denied," most likely gives both sides of the issue.
- The second article, "Plainfield Students Will Pay to Play," is about a policy that has already been approved. Therefore, it probably gives reasons for and against the policy of pay-to-play.
- The title of the third article, "Will Pay-to-Play Ruin High School Sports?" lets you know that it probably gives reasons to oppose the policy of pay-to-play.

Before you make a decision on which side of the debate to support in the issue of pay-to-play high school sports, think about the issue. How many reasons can you think of to charge students to play high school sports? Probably only one: Schools do not have enough money to fund high school sports.

Therefore, although the three articles may give some reasons to charge a fee for students who play high school sports, it appears that the best side to support in this essay is the side that opposes pay-to-play.

4. State your position on the issue of pay-to-play high school sports.

Since you know that opposing pay-to-play policies will be the easiest side to defend in your letter, let the reader know that this is your position. You should say that you *strongly oppose,* or *believe it is wrong,* or *cannot support* pay-to-pay.

5. Urge the reader to support your view and act on that support.

You might say: *I strongly encourage you to oppose the policy of pay-to-play high school sports.*

Reading the Articles

You will read the articles to find three reasons that you can use to support your stand on the issue of pay-to-play high school sports.

1. Begin reading the first article.

You are looking for reasons to oppose the policy of pay-to-play high school sports. The ninth paragraph, which begins, "True, most if not all…" contains a good reason to oppose the policy of pay-to-play. The last sentence states that the fees may be more than some families could afford to pay. Highlight this sentence and label it *#1:cost.* You now have a good first reason that you can use as information for your first body paragraph: *pay-to-play high school sports may cost too much for some families to pay.*

2. Begin reading the second article.

You are looking for a second reason to oppose the policy of pay-to-play high school sports. Read the third paragraph, which begins, " 'Parents can't afford ….' " Highlight this paragraph and label it *#1: cost* because it gives support to your first reason: the belief that some families will not be able to afford pay-to-play fees.

Continue to read and look for a second reason to oppose the policy of pay-to-play.

Read paragraph 18, which begins, "According to RHAM …." This paragraph refers to the belief that public schools are supposed to provide sports without cost to participants. Highlight and label this paragraph *#2: public education.* You now have a good second reason that you can use as information for your first body paragraph: *pay-to-play high school sports goes against the concept of public education.*

As you write your letter you will refer back to these highlighted sections.

3. Begin reading the third article.

You are looking for a third reason to support your view that pay-to-play high school sports should be opposed. Read the second paragraph, which begins, "Increasingly …," it provides two reasons to oppose the policy of pay-to-play. Highlight the phrase that claims pay-to-play is a danger to the concept of public education, and label it *#2: public education.* It provides support to your second reason that pay-to-play high school sports goes against the concept of public education.

That same sentence also contains a third reason to oppose the policy of pay-to-play high school sports: that pay-to-play will hurt the effort to get more kids involved in athletic programs. Highlight this section of the sentence and label it *#3: hurts participation.* This sentence provides a third reason to oppose pay-to-play: *pay-to-play will hurt student participation in athletic programs.*

Because your third reason was only a phrase within a sentence, it does not provide enough information to use as either quotes or support material. It is therefore necessary to read further in this article.

Notice, however, that paragraph 5, which begins "Although some schools …." does support your second reason to oppose pay-to-play. Highlight and label this sentence *#2: public education.*

While you are still searching for support information for the third reason, notice also paragraph 6, which begins, " 'It is a big issue here.' " Highlight the quote by Gayle Mulligan and label it *#1: cost* because it refers to your first argument that some families may not be able to afford pay-to-play fees.

Read the seventh paragraph, which begins, "Moreover, observers say …." The first sentence should be highlighted and labeled *#3: hurts participation.* It provides good support material for your third reason: *pay-to-play will hurt student participation in athletic programs.*

Writing the First Body Paragraph

A good body paragraph should:
- State a reason for your position
- Explain this reason
- Support it with a quote or reference to an article
- Further expand and explain the quote
- Restate your reason

1. State your first reason for opposing pay-for-play high school sports.

Your first reason to oppose pay-to-play high school sports is that many families may not be able to afford pay-to-play sports fees.

2. Explain this reason.

Look back at the three articles and find the places where you marked a *#1: cost.* Reread each of these labeled sections, and using that information, explain in your own words that
- families may not be able to pay these additional school fees.
- only families with sufficient incomes will be able to have their children participate in high school sports.
- families with several high school children or families with a child playing multiple sports will face considerable expenses.

3. Support your first reason with a quote or reference from one of the articles.
- There are several good quotes that you can choose from to show that pay-to-play policies should be opposed.
- The quote from Gayle Mulligan of Hebron, from the third article in which she states that "…would be unfair for families who could not afford them. It could make a big difference for some kids when they decide if they want to go out for a team."
- The statement in the ninth paragraph of the first article which states, "But raising participation fees could strain more family budgets, especially those families with several students eyeing high school sports."

- The statement by Kim Bettencourt in the second article in which she states, "Parents can't afford it."

Any of these would be a good reference to support your view that the policy of pay-to-play high school sports should be opposed.

4. Expand on the idea expressed in the quote or reference.

In your own words, further explain that the financial burden placed on families is a valid reason to oppose pay-to-play high school sports.

5. Restate your first reason for opposing pay-to-play high school sports.

This is the concluding sentence in your first body paragraph. It should be a restatement of your view on the issue as well as a restatement of your first reason. You might say: *Therefore, one reason to oppose pay-to-play policies is …,* or, *Clearly, pay-to-play policies can be a financial burden for many families.*

NOTE: After you have finished using information from an article, write "used" or put a check by the title of the article. This will help ensure that you use material from all three articles.

Writing the Second Body Paragraph

1. State your second reason for opposing pay-to-play high school sports.

Always begin the second and third body paragraphs with a good transition sentence, such as: *Another reason to oppose pay-to-play is …,* or, *Opposing pay-to-play is additionally important because ….*

Your second reason is pay-to-play fees violate the ideas of public education. Your opening sentence in the second body paragraph and in every body paragraph should contain your position and a reason. For example: *Another reason to oppose pay-to-play policies is that this goes against the ideas of public education.*

2. Explain this reason.

Look back at the three articles and find the places where you marked *#2: public education*. Reread each of these labeled sections, and using that information, explain in your own words that

- pay-to-play is a danger to the idea of public education.
- pay-to-play sets kids apart instead of treating all public school students equally.
- public schools are supposed to fund school sports.

3. Support the second reason with a quote or reference from one of the articles.

There are several good quotes that you can choose from to show that pay-to-play goes against the idea of public education.

- The statement about "a danger to public education" which is found in the second paragraph of the third article.
- The statement about a two-tiered system of public education which is found in the fifth paragraph of the third article. It states, parents and administrators have "...raised concern about creating a two-tier system at a public school, in which some kids have to pay, and others don't."
- The quote by the RHAM athletic director which is found in the second article. It states, "According to RHAM Athletic Director, Ed Bobinsky, the issue is simple: as a public high school, it's up to the school system to fund such activities. "Students shouldn't have to pay to play"....

Any of these would be a good reference to support your opposition to pay-to-play, which goes against the idea of public education.

4. Expand on the idea expressed in the quote or reference.

In your own words, further explain how pay-to-play policies go against the idea of public education.

5. Restate your second reason for opposing pay-to-play high school sports.

This is the concluding sentence in your second body paragraph. It should be a statement of your view on the issue as well as a restatement of your second reason. You might say, *Therefore, another reason to oppose pay-to-play high school sports is ...,* or, *Clearly, pay-to-play violates the spirit of public education.*

NOTE: After you have finished using information from an article, write "used" or put a check by the title of the article. This will help ensure that you use material from all three articles.

Writing the Third Body Paragraph

1. State your third reason for opposing pay-to-play high school sports.

Your third reason to oppose the policy of pay-to-play is that it will hurt student participation in athletic programs.

Always begin the second and third body paragraphs with a good transition sentence, such as: *Another reason to oppose pay-to-play is ...,* or, *Opposing pay-to-play is additionally important because ....*

2. Support your third reason with a quote or reference from one of the articles.

There are several good quotes that you can choose from to show pay-to-play policies should be opposed.

- The quote in the second paragraph of the third article about a drop-off in participation. It states that "...charging participation fees to be on a team...is a danger to...the overall effort to get more kids involved in athletic activities."

- The seventh paragraph of the third article discusses lower participation rates resulting from pay-to-play policies. It states, "…the implication of pay-to-play seems to lead to lower participation…"

Either of these would be a good reference to support your opposition to pay-to-play high school sports.

3. Expand on the idea expressed in the quote or reference.

In your own words, further explain how pay-to-play high school sports will reduce student participation.

4. Restate your third reason for opposing pay-to-play policies.

This is the concluding sentence in your third body paragraph. It should be a statement of your view on the issue as well as a restatement of your third reason. For example: *Therefore, another reason to oppose pay-to-play policies is …,* or, *Clearly, pay-to-play policies will hurt student participation in school sports.*

NOTE: After you have finished using information from an article, write "used" or put a check by the title of the article. This will help ensure that you use material from all three articles.

Writing the Conclusion

A good conclusion should:
- Restate your position on the issue
- List your reasons
- Urge support

1. Restate your position on the issue of pay-to-play high school sports.

You should again state that after considerable research you believe that pay-to-play high school sports should be opposed. For example: *In conclusion, it is evident that pay-to-play has no place in high school sports.* Or, *opposing pay-to-play for high school sports, therefore, is the correct choice.* Or, *the reasons to oppose pay-to-play policies far outweigh the benefits.*

2. List your reasons for opposing pay-to-play high school sports.

In this sentence you should restate the three reasons you have relied on to support your view that pay-to-play should be opposed. For example: *This policy should be opposed because …,* or, *It is essential that pay-to-play does not become high school policy because …,* or, *It is time to prevent pay-to-play because ….*

3. Urge support.

In this final sentence of the conclusion, you should ask the reader to agree with your position on the issue of pay-to-play high school sports. Some suggestions include: *Therefore, in conclusion, I ask your support in preventing pay-to-play from becoming high school policy.* Or, *I encourage you, therefore, to oppose pay-to-play high school sports. Or, these reasons should convince you that the time has come to eliminate pay-to-play policies for high school sports.*

Self-Scoring Rubric

You can estimate what kind of score you will receive on an essay by using the following self-scoring rubric. Use this tool as you practice for the writing test. Look at each category. Circle the description in each category that best applies to your essay letter. You should have twelve circles when you have finished scoring your essay. Where do most of your scores fall? Three? Four? Five? Six?

Remember: Even if the rest of your eleven scores on these rubrics are fives and sixes, the scorers can rarely give you higher than a final score of four if you do not use all three sources.

Self-Scoring Rubric

	Categories	Three	Four	Five	Six
1	**Takes a stand**	yes, but not clearly developed	yes	yes	yes
2	**Persuasiveness**	not a very persuasive stand	somewhat persuasive	persuasive	very persuasive
3	**Awareness of audience**	some awareness	some awareness	awareness is evident	very aware
4	**Support**	some support	adequate support	well supported	richly supported
5	**Use of sources**	not all 3 sources used	not all 3 sources used	all 3 sources used	all 3 sources used
6	**Development of ideas**	few ideas are developed	adequately developed	well developed	very well developed
7	**Accuracy of information**	some inaccuracies/ irrelevant	some inaccuracies/ irrelevant	yes	yes
8	**Organization/ focus**	somewhat	adequate	well organized	very well organized
9	**Ideas**	not always clear	most ideas are clear	clearly expressed	clear and effective
10	**Flow of ideas**	choppy flow of thought	ideas and writing flow	generally flow	very fluent
11	**Transition**	lacking transitions	some transitions	good transitions	effective transitions
12	**Length**	less than 2 pages	2 pages	2½ pages	3 full pages

Practice Test Two—Interdisciplinary Writing Test

Issue Two

Overview

The purpose of this interdisciplinary writing test is to determine how well you can write to persuade others to think as you do about an issue. In this test, you will read a few short articles about an important issue, take a position on the issue and write a first draft of a persuasive letter. You must support your position with information from *each* of the source materials. Your response will be read and scored by trained readers.

About This Test

In this Interdisciplinary Writing test, you will think about and take a position on an important issue: **whether schools should be prohibited from using Native-American names for teams and mascots.** While you are working on this test, you will use skills and knowledge you learned in your language arts, mathematics, science, social studies, the arts, and other classes.

The Issue

In recent years, controversy has arisen over the use of Indian and Native-American names for high school teams and mascots. Because of increased and renewed protest, some people believe that Indian and Native-American names should be changed for high school teams and mascots. Those opposed to the team name and mascot changes argue Indian and Native-American names are positive symbols of pride and character.

Article One

Name-Calling

Debating the Future of Native American Sports Team Mascots

What's in a name? Plenty—especially if you're a sports fan. Your favorite team's name and mascot (a person, an animal, or a cartoon character that represents a team) send a message about how the team hopes to be viewed by others. For example, the name of the San Francisco 49ers professional football team and its mascot recall the adventurous days of the 1849 California gold rush.

Some team names and mascots are based on ethnic groups; what about them? According to the National Coalition on Racism in Sports & Media, more than 4,000 U.S. schools and colleges currently use Native American team names and mascots. Some people say using mascots based on ethnicity is insulting. Others, however, say Native American-based mascots are meant to be viewed as symbols of honor and pride.

Illinois Controversy

The question about using Native American mascots was recently debated at Niles West High School in Skokie, Ill. On October 16, the Niles West school board voted to change the mascot from an "Indian," the school's mascot since the 1950s.

The decision to change the high school mascot was not an easy one. Before the school board meeting, students at Niles West High School had voted on the issue. Sixty-seven percent of students voted in favor of keeping the mascot. That didn't stop the school board, however, from voting 6 to 1 to change the mascot.

An Insult or an Honor?

Many people who favored changing the mascot said the symbol is degrading and offensive to Native Americans. Matthew Beaudet, president of the Illinois Native American Bar Association, said, "[Native Americans] are not a trophy to be hung up on a wall. This does not honor us."

Jordan Feder, a Niles West senior and president of the student senate, agrees. "[Using the Indian mascot] is something that should not be done. It's shameful that this has been going on for so long," Feder said.

People in favor of the Native American mascot, however, disagree. Richard Witry, a Skokie historian, said the Indian mascot was not meant to be offensive, but to symbolize a local heritage. "This is an area that was heavily populated with the Potawatomi Indians .... There is a strong Indian tradition in this area."

Roy Swenson, a 1958 Niles West graduate, agrees. Swenson said, "We should be proud of the mascots that we have. There is nothing disrespectful about the Indians."

Should schools stop using Native American-based sports team names and mascots?

Article Two

AKRON BEACON JOURNAL

Ruling Could Affect Teams with Native American Mascots

BY DAVID ADAMS

Watch out Wahoo.

With the Washington Redskins' name and logo challenged by the U.S. Patent and Trademark Office, could the Cleveland Indians' name and toothy Chief Wahoo mascot be far behind?

On Friday, the government agency responsible for policing exclusive rights stripped the National Football League team of its exclusive right to use the name and logo because it is derogatory to Native Americans.

While the ruling does not prevent the Redskins from using the name or logo, it would allow anyone else to use it at no cost.

The ultimate effect of the ruling is unclear. It is not known whether the ruling extends to the names and logos of other sports teams such as the Indians, the Chicago Blackhawks, the Atlanta Braves or the Kansas City Chiefs. Also, the Redskins' legal team said they are likely to appeal the ruling.

But the prospect of open season on Native American names and logos is scary news to investors who own stock in the publicly traded Cleveland Indians.

The team's widely recognized name and mascot are known around the world.

Last year, the team made $1.5 million from the sale of licensed merchandise, and about $15 million in revenue from sales at its team shops, including ones in Belden Village, Jacobs Field and the Galleria in downtown Cleveland.

The team's exclusive license requires companies that use the Indians' trademarks in any way to pay a portion of their revenue to Major League Baseball and, indirectly, the Indians.

Team spokesman Robert DiBiasio said Monday that the team was studying the patent and trademark office's ruling, and had no comment.

Trademark officials also declined to comment.

But the agency's ruling—while scary for Indians' investors—is a relief for Cleveland-based Native American groups who have petitioned—even protested—for years against continued use of the Indians' name and logo.

Robert Roche of the American Indian Movement said the ruling gives momentum and exposure to his group's fight. He said it shows that he and others are not alone when they say that the use of the name and logo is demeaning.

"We're not mascots. We're a race of people," said Roche of Cleveland.

"If you have a [team named the] Cleveland African-Americans with a mascot with a bone in the nose, or a [team named the] Cleveland Jews with a mascot wearing a yarmulke, you'd have a war up here."

The ruling should be precedential, said Juan Reyna, chairman of the Cleveland-based Committee of 500 Years of Dignity and Resistance.

"If that ruling is against the Redskins, I don't see how it wouldn't apply to the Indians, the Braves, the Chiefs and the Blackhawks," said Reyna of Cleveland. "It's about time the consciousness of this country has woken up to include indigenous people who have the right not to be humiliated and degraded."

That push for sensitivity in sports teams names and mascots is working, at least on the college sports level. Recently, Ohio's Miami University changed its name from the Redskins to the Redhawks, and St. John's University in New York changed its name from the Redmen to the Red Storm.

The U.S. Patent and Trademark office in Washington said the use of the Redskins name and logo was derogatory. The office brushed aside counter claims by the team that people who used Redskins were referring only to the football team.

Native American groups that filed the complaint alleged that the word Redskins "has been and is used with connotations of violence, savagery, and oppression; and that the usage suggests a power relationship ... connecting Indians with savagery."

The team argued that no disparagement was intended, and that its use "reflected positive attributes of the American Indian such as dedication, courage and pride, such as its use on the nickel."

The team was originally located in Boston and known as the Boston Braves. In 1933 the team was renamed the Boston Redskins. When the team moved to Washington, D.C., in 1937, it was renamed the Washington Redskins.

In perhaps the most significant aspect of the Redskins case for the Cleveland Indians, expert testimony showed that many Native Americans felt more strongly against "Redskins" than they did against "Indians." Forty-six percent of those surveyed said they found "Redskins" offensive, while more than 7 percent found "Indians" offensive.

The Indians' team has claimed the team name is meant to honor former player Louis Sockalexis. And while the team has laid low during the sporadic complaints directed at its name and mascot, current majority owner Richard Jacobs has said the team intends to keep the two.

The Indians' merchandise is among the most popular in all of Major League Baseball, ranking behind the New York Yankees.

Money made from the sale of licensed merchandise is collected by Major League Baseball Properties, and then redistributed evenly among all major league teams.

Article Three

SAN DIEGO UNION-TRIBUNE   THE MORNING STAR INSTITUTE

Should High Schools Use Indian Names for Their Sports Teams?

Hundreds of school teams have Indian names. Some say it's offensive to root for the "Redskins." Others say lighten up, no harm intended.

YES

LeBron James, the nation's most celebrated high school basketball player, and his team, the St. Vincent–St. Mary Fighting Irish of Akron, Ohio, recently played in Los Angeles: Roughly 13 percent of California's population is Irish-American; but there were no protests because the Irish-American community saw nothing particularly offensive about the Akron high school's team name.

That's why it's hard to understand the crusade to outlaw the use of Indian-related team names and mascots by public schools. Last year, a California legislator proposed banning the use of Redskins, Indians, Braves, Chiefs, Apaches, Comanches, or any other American Indian tribal name. A similar measure has been proposed in the U.S. House of Representatives.

Had the California law been enacted, the state's 60 or more public schools and colleges that boast Indian team names would have been forced to abandon those monikers. But the bill was based on the dubious notion that Indian team names make life unbearable for American Indians.

It assumes that most American Indians find such team names and mascots racially offensive.

But that's not true, according to a poll last year, conducted for *Sports Illustrated.* "Although most Native American activists and tribal leaders consider Indian team names and mascots offensive, neither Native Americans in general, nor a cross-section of U.S. sports fans agree," says Andrea Woo of *Sports Illustrated.* In fact, four of five American Indians said that professional teams (like the Washington Redskins) should not stop using Indian names. Asked whether the use of Indian nicknames contributes to discrimination against them, the vast majority said it does not.

Actually, Indian team names foment goodwill toward American Indians. They are positive symbols in the minds of students. Teams like the Kansas City Chiefs and the Atlanta Braves are the pride of their cities.

When it comes to team names and team mascots, intent is what matters. Are they meant to disparage a group of people? Or do they represent inspirational symbols around which fans of all backgrounds can rally? Most American Indians understand the distinction. Too bad those who presume to speak for them do not.

Reprinted with permission of Joseph Perkins, Columnist, *San Diego Union-Tribune*

NO

The overwhelming majority of Native Americans despise "Indian" sports references and want all schools to put an end to this tradition of recreational racism.

Even if you think your school shows the greatest respect for your team, there are always the opposing fans being disrespectful—to your name and symbols. When effigies of Indians are burned in bonfires, or when signs and chants call for Indians to be scalped and tomahawked, Native people—especially students—take those insults personally.

Such behaviors promote assaults against living Indian people and have no proper place in the American educational system or public arena. The sports names that draw from a specific Native nation, such as Apache or Cherokee, steal and debase their very identity. The only teams with a right to use tribal names are those whose players are citizens of that tribal nation. That's self-identification.

There are no teams called Zulus or French or Japanese, but there are hundreds of non-Native teams with tribal names. What about the "Fighting Irish"? That came from the original all-Irish players, not from any outsiders. And how about "Cowboys"? That's a profession, not a people.

The use of Native references in sports amounts to name-calling. It reduces the entire race to caricatures at a time when health and poverty problems in Indian country need to be addressed with utmost seriousness.

All the leading Native American organizations have called for an end to Native-related names and images in sports. So have the National Education Association, the U.S. Commission on Civil Rights, and hundreds of social-justice and religious groups nationwide.

In 1970, the first "Indian" mascot was retired—the University of Oklahoma's "Little Red." At that time, there were more than 3,000 American schools using Indian names and symbols for their sports teams. Today, there are fewer than 1,200. American society is changing for the better, and it's high time for the rest of the schools to get on the right side of history.

—Suzan Shown Harjo, President, *The Morning Star Institute,* (Native American rights group) Reprinted with permission.

How to Write This Persuasive Essay

Writing the Introduction

As you now know, a good introduction must:
- State the issue
- Show how it is controversial
- Show that you are an expert on the topic
- Take a stand
- Urge support

Reading the Directions

Before the start of this test, the teacher will read several pages of directions and ask you to follow along. This time is *not* part of your 65 minute test time. However, you can use this direction time to begin gathering information that you can later use in your persuasive letter.

The Issue

What Is the Issue?

In the actual Test Booklet on page 4, there is a section entitled "About this Test". In this paragraph you will find a sentence in bold print. As our teacher reads this section to you during the direction part of the test, use your **highlighter** to mark the bold print sentence that follows the phrase "take a position on an important issue:"

When you begin to write your letter, you can copy that sentence exactly into your introductory paragraph. This will prevent you from incorrectly stating the issue.

How Is It Controversial?

You will also find on page 4 of the actual Test Booklet, a section entitled "The Issue." As your teacher reads this paragraph to you during the directions, **highlight** the two sentences that show the controversial nature of the issue. The sentences always include the phrases "some people believe..." and "those opposed to the idea argue..." You can use these two sentences from the directions in your introduction to show your understanding of the topic.

To Whom Do I Write?

In the actual Test Booklet on page 5, there is a section entitled "Your Task". As your teacher reads this paragraph to you during the directions, look at the first bold print sentence. It says **"You will read a** few articles about..., take a position on the issue and write a persuasive letter to..." **Highlight** the person or group to whom you are to write your letter.

The Salutation

Begin your letter with "Dear," followed by the name of the person or group that you highlighted in the directions. For example, you can use *Dear Governor,* or *Dear Representative,* or *Dear Forest Service.*

Time

In the directions that your teacher will read to you during the test is a section entitled, "Organizing Your Time." It is suggested that you break up your 65 minutes into 2 parts: 30 minutes for reading and 35 minutes for writing your letter. Most students, however, choose not to follow that approach. Instead, it is far easier to begin writing your introduction immediately, decide your position on the issue, then read just enough information from each article to find material and quotes to support your position on the issue.

1. **Begin your introduction with the statement of the issue, exactly as it appears in the test directions section called "*About This Test.*"**

   Some suggestions include:
   - Prohibiting the use of Native American names for teams and mascots is a controversial issue across the country.
   - An issue that is often debated today is the use of Native American names for teams and mascots.
   - The proposal to prohibit the use of Native American names for teams and mascots has received much attention recently.

2. **Show the reader how this issue is controversial.**

   To do this, use the two sentences that you highlighted in the section called "The Issue." You may paraphrase the sentences in your own words or use the wording in the test booklet.

   Some suggestions include:
   - Because of increased and renewed protest, some people believe that Indian and Native American names should be changed for high school teams and mascots. Those opposed to the team name and mascot changes argue Indian and Native-American names are positive symbols of pride and character.
   - The debate over the use of Native American names for high school teams and mascots is between those who believe that the time has come to heed the protests and change the names and those who argue that these names are positive symbols.
   - Those who favor ending the use of Native American names for high school teams and mascots believe that schools should heed the protest of Native Americans while those who favor keeping the names argue that these names are a sign of pride and character.

3. Show that you are an expert on the topic.

To do this, write that you have read several articles concerning the issue of using Native American names for teams and mascots. Some suggestions include:

- I have read several articles on the topic of prohibiting the use of Native American names for teams and mascots.
- I have researched this topic.
- I have investigated the issue of Native American names for teams and mascots.

Finally, it is time to look at the three articles to decide which side of the issue you will support. Read the title of each article and any bold-print headings. If there are no bold-print headings in the article, read the first paragraph. This will usually give you a hint as to which side of the debate the article will present.

- The title of the first article, "Name Calling," tells you that it probably opposes the use of Native American names for teams and mascots.
- The second article tells about a court decision, so it probably gives reasons why Native American names should not be used.
- The third article clearly intends to show both sides of the issue.

Therefore, although the three articles may give some reasons to continue the use of Native-American names for teams and mascots, it appears that the best side to support in this essay is the side that favors prohibiting their use.

4. State your position on the issue of using Native American names for teams and mascots.

Since you know that supporting an end to their use will be the easiest side to defend in your letter, let the reader know that this is your position. You should say that you strongly oppose or are against the use of Native American names for teams and mascots.

5. Urge the reader to support your view and act on that support.

You might say, "I recommend that you support an end to use of Native American names for teams and mascots."

Reading the Articles

You will read the articles to find three reasons that you can use to support your stand on the issue of using Native American names for teams and mascots.

1. Begin reading the first article.

You are looking for the first reason to prohibit the use of Native American names for teams and mascots.

The second paragraph contains a sentence that will provide your first reason. The fourth sentence states that "Some people say using mascots based on ethnicity is insulting." Highlight this sentence and label it *#1: disrespectful.* You now have your first reason to oppose the use of Native American names by high school teams and mascots: *It is disrespectful.* Because this is one simple sentence without any support information, you should read further to find more material and quotes.

Paragraph 6, which begins, "Jordan Feder ...," should be highlighted and labeled *#1: disrespect,* because he states that using Native American names "...is something that should not be done. It is shameful that this has been going on for so long."

You now have enough information and quotes to support your first reason to oppose the use of Native American names by high school teams and mascots: *It is disrespectful.*

2. Begin reading the second article.

You are looking for a second reason to prohibit the use of Native American names for teams and mascots.

Read paragraph 13, which begins, "But the agency's ruling...." Highlight and label paragraph 13 *#1: many Native Americans oppose it* because it supports your first reason when it refers to the many groups that have petitioned and protested the use of these names.

Read paragraph 14, which begins "Robert Roche..." The second sentence indicates that the use of Native American names for teams and mascots is disrespectful. Highlight this sentence and label it *#2: many Native Americans oppose it.*

You now have a second reason to oppose the use of Native-American names by high school teams and mascots: *many Native Americans oppose it.*

3. Begin reading the third article.

You immediately notice that this particular article gives both sides of the issue. Since you have already decided to oppose the use of Native American names for high school teams and mascots, skip the first section of the article because it supports keeping the names.

As you read the "NO" column, you are looking for a third reason to prohibit the use of Native American names by high school teams and mascots. Remember, however, that you may find information and quotes that will support your first two reasons.

For example, in the first paragraph, highlight the first sentence, label it *#2: many Native Americans oppose it.* This sentence supports your second reason that the use of these names is opposed by most Native Americans.

The second paragraph also gives support to your first reason. Highlight the paragraph and label it *#1: disrespectful* because it shows how the use of these names can lead to disrespect by fans from opposing schools.

The third paragraph finally contains a third reason to oppose the use of Native American names for teams and mascots. The last two sentences should be highlighted because they make the point that only teams made up of Native Americans have the right to use Native American names for their teams and mascots. For anyone else to use these names is to steal the identity of Native Americans. Label these sentences *#3: only Native American players.* Now you have a third reason to prohibit the use of Native American names for teams and mascots: *they should be used only by teams made up of Native American players.*

Writing the First Body Paragraph

A good body paragraph should:
- State a reason for your position
- Explain this reason
- Support it with a quote or reference to an article
- Further expand and explain the quote
- Restate your reason

1. **State your first reason for supporting the view that teams and mascots should be prohibited from using Native American names.**

   Your first reason is that the use of Native American names for teams and mascots is disrespectful. Your opening sentence in the first body paragraph and in every body paragraph should contain your position and a reason: *One reason to prohibit the use of Native American names for teams and mascots is that it is disrespectful.*

2. **Explain this reason.**

   Look back at the three articles and find the places where you marked *#1: disrespectful.* Reread each of these labeled sections. Now, using that information explain in your own words that
   - the use of these names is insulting
   - the use of these names is shameful
   - fans from opposing teams often disrespect the image of the Native American mascot
   - these names have no place in a public school because they are disrespectful

3. **Support the first reason with a quote or reference from one of the articles.**

   There are several good quotes that you can choose from to show that the use of Native American names by high school teams and mascots is disrespectful.

   Some suggestions include:
   - The statement in the first article, paragraph 6, in which Jordan Feder states that using Native American names "…is something that should not be done. It is shameful that this has been going on for so long."
   - The statement in the third article, about the opposing fans that describe their insulting actions toward the mascots of teams using Native American names.
   - The statement in the third article that these names "…have no proper place in the American educational system."

   Any of these would be a good reference to support your view that the use of Native American names for teams and mascots should be prohibited because they show disrespect.

4. Expand on the idea expressed in the quote or reference.

In your own words, further explain how the use of Native American names by high school teams and mascots is disrespectful.

5. Restate your first reason for opposing the use of Native-American names for teams and mascots.

This is the concluding sentence in your first body paragraph. It should be a statement of your view on the issue as well as a restatement of your first reason. You might say: *Therefore, one reason to oppose the use of Native American names for teams and mascots is…,* or, *Clearly, prohibiting the use of Native American names for teams and mascots should be prohibited because it is disrespectful.*

NOTE: After you have finished using information from an article, write "used" or put a check by the title of the article. This will help ensure that you use material from all three articles.

Writing the Second Body Paragraph

1. State your second reason for prohibiting the use of Native American names for teams and mascots.

Always begin the second and third body paragraphs with a good transition sentence. Some suggestions include: *Another reason to prohibit the use of Native American names for teams and mascots is…,* or, *Prohibiting the use of Native American names for teams and mascots is additionally important because….*

Your second reason to prohibit the use of Native American names is because many Native Americans oppose it.

2. Explain this reason.

Look back at the three articles and find all the places where you marked *#2: many Native Americans oppose it.*

Reread each of these labeled sections, and using that information explain in your own words that

- many Native American groups have petitioned and protested this use of their names.
- the vast majority of Native Americans despise "Indian" sports references
- most Native Americans want to end this tradition of recreational racism.

3. Support your second reason with a quote or reference from one of the articles.

There are several good quotes that you can choose from to show that many Native Americans oppose the use of their names for teams and mascots.

Some suggestions include:

- the statement in the second article that states "…the agency's ruling…is a relief for Cleveland-based Native American groups who have petitioned—even protested—for years against the use of the Indians' name and logo."
- the opening statement in the second section of the third article which states, "The overwhelming majority of Native Americans despise "Indian" sports references…"

Either of these would be a good reference to support your view that the use of Native-American names for teams and mascots should be prohibited.

4. Expand on the ideas expressed in the quote or reference.

In your own words, further explain why Native Americans oppose the use of their name for team names and mascots.

5. Restate your second reason for prohibiting the use of Native American names for teams and mascots.

This is the concluding sentence in your second body paragraph. It should be a statement of your view on the issue as well as a restatement of your second reason. For example: *Therefore, another reason to prohibit the use of Native American names for teams and mascots is…,* or, *Clearly, most Native Americans oppose the use of their names for teams and mascots.*

NOTE: After you have finished using information from an article, write "used" or put a check by the title of the article. This will help ensure that you use material from all three articles.

Writing the Third Body Paragraph

1. State your third reason for prohibiting the use of Native American names for teams and mascots.

Remember to begin the second and third body paragraphs with a good transition sentence. Some suggestions include: *Another reason to prohibit the use of Native American names for teams and mascots is …,* or, *Prohibiting teams and mascots from using Native American names is additionally important because ….*

Your third reason to oppose the use of Native American names for teams and mascots is that the only teams that have the right to use these names are those made up of Native American players.

2. Explain this reason.

Look back at the three articles and find the places where you marked a *#3*. Reread each of these labeled sections, and using that information, explain in your own words that
- only teams composed of Native American players can use Native American names.
- others who use these names are stealing the identity of Native Americans.

3. Support your third reason with a quote or reference from one of the articles.

There are several good quotes that you can choose from to show that many Native Americans oppose the use of their names for teams and mascots.

Some suggestions include:
- The statement in the third article that says, "The only teams with a right to use tribal names are those whose players are citizens of that tribal nation."
- The statement in the third article that states that the use of Native American names should be only for Native Americans because it is "self-identification."

4. Expand on the idea expressed in the quote or reference.

In your own words, further explain why only teams composed of Native Americans have the right to use Native American names for teams and mascots.

5. Restate your third reason for prohibiting the use of Native American names for teams and mascots.

This is the concluding sentence in your third body paragraph. It should be a restatement of your view on the issue as well as a restatement of your third reason. For example: *Therefore, another reason to prohibit the use of Native American names for teams and mascots is ...,* or, *Clearly, only teams composed of Native American players have the right to use Native-American names for teams and mascots.*

NOTE: After you have finished using information from an article, write "used" or put a check by the title of the article. This will help ensure that you use material from all three articles.

Writing the Conclusion

A good conclusion should:
- Restate your position on the issue
- List your reasons
- Urge support

1. **Restate your position on the issue of using Native American names for teams and mascots.**

   You should again state that after considerable research you believe that teams and mascots should be prohibited from using Native American names. You might say: *It is obvious, therefore, that Native American names should not be used by teams and mascots.* Or, *Prohibiting the use of Native American names by teams and mascots is the right thing to do.*

2. **List your reasons for prohibiting the use of Native American names by teams and mascots.**

   In this sentence you should restate the three reasons you have relied on to support your view that Native American names should not be used for teams or mascots. Some suggestions include: *Teams and mascots should not use these names because ...,* Or, *Native American names are not appropriate for teams and mascots because ....*

3. **Urge support.**

   In this final sentence of the conclusion, you should ask the reader to agree with your position to prohibit the use of Native American names for teams and mascots. For example: *In conclusion, I ask your support of a prohibition on the use of Native American names for teams and mascots.* Or, *These reasons should convince you that the time has come to prohibit the use of Native American names for teams and mascots.*

Self-Scoring Rubric

   You can estimate what kind of score you will receive on an essay by using the following self-scoring rubric. Use this tool as you practice for the writing test. Look at each category. Circle the description in each category that best applies to your essay letter. You should have twelve circles when you have finished scoring your essay. Where do most of your scores fall? Three? Four? Five? Six?

Remember: Even if the rest of your eleven scores on these rubrics are fives and sixes, the scorers can give you no higher than a final score of four if you do not use all three sources.

Self-Scoring Rubric

	Categories	Three	Four	Five	Six
1	**Takes a stand**	yes, but not clearly developed	yes	yes	yes
2	**Persuasiveness**	not a very persuasive stand	somewhat persuasive	persuasive	very persuasive
3	**Awareness of audience**	some awareness	some awareness	awareness is evident	very aware
4	**Support**	some support	adequate support	well supported	richly supported
5	**Use of sources**	not all 3 sources used	not all 3 sources used	all 3 sources used	all 3 sources used
6	**Development of ideas**	few ideas are developed	adequately developed	well developed	very well developed
7	**Accuracy of information**	some inaccuracies/ irrelevant	some inaccuracies/ irrelevant	yes	yes
8	**Organization/ focus**	somewhat	adequate	well organized	very well organized
9	**Ideas**	not always clear	most ideas are clear	clearly expressed	clear and effective
10	**Flow of ideas**	choppy flow of thought	ideas and writing flow	generally flow	very fluent
11	**Transition**	lacking transitions	some transitions	good transitions	effective transitions
12	**Length**	less than 2 pages	2 pages	2½ pages	3 full pages

In this test you are asked to edit and review examples of student writing. It measures your ability to use standard written English as well as to improve sentences. During this test you will read several passages and look for embedded errors and answer multiple choice questions to indicate appropriate corrections.

This test will focus on your knowledge and skills in the following specific areas.

Composing and Revising

A. *Content, Organization, and Tone* including topic sentence, supporting detail, extraneous material, logical order, tone and redundancy of ideas

B. *Revision: Syntax* including fragment, run-on; awkward construction, parallel construction and sentence combining

C. *Revision: Word Choice* including descriptive language, transition words, generality/specificity and misplaced modifiers

Editing

A. *Capitalization* including titles of people, proper nouns, proper adjectives, first word in dialogue and names of places, organizations, nationalities, buildings, historical events and works of art

B. *Punctuation* including the use of the comma, quotation marks, apostrophe, semicolon and colon

C. *Usage* including subject and verb agreement, verb tense, pronoun reference, pronoun case, indefinite pronoun, special problems in usage and adjective/adverb usage

D. *Spelling*

In this test, the lines in each passage are numbered. This is to help you refer back to specific parts of the passage as you answer the questions. As you read each question, it is helpful to highlight the lines or words that are referred to in each question.

Remember the test has 3 passages, each with six questions and you are allowed 25 minutes for this test. Therefore, you should allow about 8 minutes for reading and answering the questions in each passage.

Each test in this section contains 3 passages, 18 questions on editing and revising as well as explanations of the correct answers.

Set your timer for 25 minutes and begin.

Read the following articles and answer the multiple-choice questions. You will have 25 minutes to complete this test.

Passage One

TRANSPORTATION CONSULTANT

A local nonprofit organization has written this letter to a state official asking for the transportation board commissioner to consider hiring an outside consultant. Read the letter, then answer the multiple-choice questions that follow.

1   The Scenic Roads Project respectfully asks that you send a letter to
2   the Transportation Board Commissioner. We suggest that the Commissioner hire
3   an outside designer/engineer with expertese in designing roads in environmentally
4   sensitive corridors.
5   At this point, the Transportation Board is in the process of finalizing plans
6   for the improvement of two sections of the road in question. To date, however,
7   none of the plans presented has shown any sensitivity for the valuable historical,
8   scenic and environmental resources of the corridor. Preliminary plans reflect a
9   cookie-cutter, one-size-fits-all approach to making the road safer and improving
10 traffic flow. The "bigger is better" premise behind the solutions presented thus far
11 is outmoded and expensive. It will cost unnecessary tax dollars and destroy the
12 unique rural character of the corridor. This is not the place for an alternative truck
13 route to the nearby Interstate. We know that local anglers like the fishing
14 opportunities the two lane bridges provide. A divided four-lane highway will
15 lower air and water quality, endanger farming in the area, and limited potential
16 for heritage tourism.
17   After consulting with an internationally recognized transportation
18 engineer, the Scenic Roads Project is convinced that the history, the
19 environmental health, and the scenic nature of the corridor are valuable
20 resources that don't have to be sacrificed. Safe, scenic, modernized roads have
21 been designed and build in other parts of the country. With the help and expertise
22 of a recognized road designer working with the Transportation Board engineers,
23 we can preserve the character of our area and at the same time, build a road that
24 will meet current and future needs.

Passage 1 Questions

1. What is the best change, if any, to make to the sentence in lines 2–4 (*We ... corridors.*)?
   a. Change *expertese* to **expertise.**
   b. Change *corridors* to **corradors.**
   c. Change *hire* to **hires.**
   d. Make no change.

2. What is the best change, if any, to make to the sentence in lines 10–11 (*The ... expensive.*)?
   a. Change *premise* to **promise.**
   b. Change *thus far* to **thusly.**
   c. Change *outmoded* to **of an old style.**
   d. Make no change.

3. The sentence that does not belong in this passage is the sentence in
   a. lines 5–6 (*At ... question.*)
   b. lines 13–14 (*We ...provide.*)
   c. lines 13–16 (*A ... tourism.*)
   d. lines 20–21 (*Safe ... country.*)

4. What is the best change, if any, to make to the sentence in lines 14–16 (*A ... tourism.*)?
   a. Change *heritage* to **heritige.**
   b. Insert a semicolon after *quality.*
   c. Change *limited* to **limit.**
   d. Make no change.

5. What is the best change, if any, to make to the sentence in lines 20–21 (*Safe ... country.*)?
   a. Change *roads* to **road's.**
   b. Insert a semicolon after *designed.*
   c. Change *build* to **built.**
   d. Make no change.

6. What is the best way to change the sentence in lines 21–24 (*With … needs.*)?

   a. With the help and expertise of a recognized road designer working with the Transportation Board engineers, we can preserve the character of our area and build a road that will meet current and future needs.

   b. With help and expertise, a recognized road designer working with the Transportation Board engineers, we can preserve the character of our area and build a road that will meet current and future needs.

   c. With the help and expertise of a recognized road designer; working with the Transportation Board engineers, we can preserve the character of our area and build a road that will meet current and future needs.

   d. With the help and expertise of a recognized road designer we can preserve the character of our area and build a road that will meet current and future needs of the Transportation Board engineers.

Passage Two

SWEET MEMORIES

Sarah has written this essay for her creative writing class. It describes the relationship of a woman and her mother-in-law. Read the essay, then answer the multiple-choice questions that follow.

1 Its a weekend in May as we sit here at the dining room table, and I'm
2 puffed up about the lemon poppy seed cake I've made to serve over the weekend.
3 My confidence in the tasty bundt cake is its humbel origins in two boxes
4 of commercial muffin mix. Skittish in the kitchen, I cling to this cake recipe
5 that I've only burned once. Even if the cake is based in muffin mix, the
6 powdered sugar glaze is good enough to make anything taste good. I boast of the
7 cake's reliability, as if the solid base of muffin mix was part of my hand in it.
8 When I get fancy, I add a squeeze of lemon juice. Sometimes from an actual
9 lemon, not the hard plastic kind.
10 She recalled making a cake with freshly grated coconut, and how the
11 extra effort made the cake so delicious. That same day, the power went
12 out, so the cake was served in place of dinner and was then known as the
13 Lakin Blackout Cake. How many cakes has she made in a lifetime? Yet, she can
14 remember the steps, the ingredients, the flavors, and describe them in such a way
15 that even a confirmed coconut hater is hungry for a taste of the Lakin Blackout
16 Cake.
17 Her skills have been honed on the daily exertions of making family life
18 enjoyable who wouldn't be handy in the kitchen after two decades of making
19 meals for six? But her talents, to my eyes, have something of a magical quality.
20 Like the way fitted sheets can be folded into a neat square, instead of a wad of
21 fabric wedged into the linen closet. Even the simple act of making a cake
22 becomes a memorable event, rather than a rote stirring of pre-mixed ingredients.

Passage 2 Questions

1. What is the best change, if any, to make to the sentence in lines 1–2 (*Its ... weekend.*)?
   a. Change *Its* to **It's.**
   b. Change *dining* to **dinning.**
   c. Add a comma after *made.*
   d. Make no change.

2. What is the best change to make to the sentence in lines 3–4 (*My ... mix.*)?
   a. Change *its* to **it's.**
   b. Change *humbel* to **humble.**
   c. Change *commercial* to **comercial.**
   d. Make no change.

3. What is the best way to change the sentence in lines 6–7 (*I ... it.*)?
   a. I boast of the cake's reliability, as if I'd had a hand in making the muffin mix.
   b. I boast of the cake's reliability, the muffin mix being solid as a hand.
   c. I boast of the cake's reliability, the muffin mix like an extra hand.
   d. I boast of the cake's reliability, although the muffin mix makes it solid.

4. What is the best way to correct the fragment in lines 8–9 (*When ... kind.*)?
   a. When I get fancy, I add a squeeze of fresh lemon juice to the batter.
   b. When I get fancy, I add a squeeze of lemon juice from a real lemon, instead of the concentrated lemon juice packaged in a hard plastic lemon.
   c. Lemon juice makes the batter fancy, even if it is just from reconstituted lemon juice.
   d. When I get fancy; I add a squeeze of real lemon juice to the batter.

5. What it the best change, if any, to make to the sentence in lines 10–11 (*She ... delicious.*)?
   a. Insert a comma after *freshly.*
   b. Changed *recalled* to **recalling.**
   c. Change *delicious* to **deliciously.**
   d. Make no change.

6. What is the best way to change the sentence in lines 17–19 (*Her ... six?*)?
   a. Insert a comma after *honed.*
   b. Insert a colon after *exertions.*
   c. Insert a semicolon after *enjoyable.*
   d. Insert a comma after *kitchen.*

Passage Three

NATIONAL HIGHWAYS

Cameron has written this essay for her history class. It explains the development of federally funded highways. Read the essay, then answer the multiple-choice questions that follow.

1   Systematic federal assistance for highways began in 1916, with grants to
2   states for construction of roads used to deliver the mail. Roads receiving federal
3   highway aid were to be free of toles, and all proposed roads and methods of
4   construction had to be agreed on by the Secretary of Agriculture and state
5   highway departments.
6   Federal and state investment's of more than $8 billion in the 1920s and
7   1930s boosted total mileage of paved roads from 387,000 in 1921 to 1.4 million
8   by 1940. During World War II, appropriations for roads needed for national
9   defense, including access to military sites, funded hundreds more projects.
10   Now, in the year 2003, commuters swarm metropolitan roads every workday.
11   In each of the first 3 postwar years, $500 million in federal funds was
12   authorized for construction and funding of secondary roads to connect farms and
13   small communities to the highway network and an urban system located in and
14   around major citys. An Interstate highway system was designed for connecting
15   big cities and industrial centers and connecting with routes in Canada and
16   Mexico. Today's highway system, while retaining marks of all this history, is
17   overlaid by legislation passed in 1956 authorizing completion of the Interstate
18   system under the direction of the Department of Commerce and state highway
19   departments. To make things go faster, the system was to have no railroad
20   crossings, traffic signals, or stop signs. In 1988, the system was 99 percent
21   complete and had consisted of 44, 590 miles.

Passage Three Questions

1. What is the best change to make, if any, to the sentence in lines 2–5 (*Roads … departments.*)?
   a. Insert a comma after *aid*.
   b. Change *toles* to **tolls.**
   c. Insert a colon after *by*.
   d. Make no change.

2. What is the best change, if any, to make in lines 6–8 (*Federal … 1940.*)?
   a. Change *investment's* to **investments.**
   b. Change *paved* to **paving.**
   c. Insert a semicolon after *roads*.
   d. Make no change.

3. The sentence that does not belong in this passage is the sentence in
   a. lines 1–2 (*Systematic … mail.*).
   b. line 10 (*Now…workday.*).
   c. lines 14–16 (*An … Mexico.*).
   d. lines 20–21 (*In … miles.*).

4. What is the best change to make to the sentence in lines 11–14 (*In … cities.*)?
   a. Insert a comma after *million*.
   b. Change *funds* to **fund's.**
   c. Change *urban* to **urbane.**
   d. Change *citys* to **cities.**

5. What is the best change, if any, to make to the sentence in lines 16–19 (*Today's … departments.*)?
   a. Change *retaining* to **retainment.**
   b. Change *overlaid* to **waylaid.**
   c. Change *authorizing* to **authorized.**
   d. Make no change.

6. What is the best way to change the sentence in lines 19–20 (*To make … signs.*)?
  a. To build the road quickly, the system was to have no railroad crossings, traffic signals, or stop signs.
  b. To keep traffic moving, the system was to have no railroad crossings, traffic signals, or stop signs.
  c. To save money, the system was to have no railroad crossings, traffic signals, or stop signs.
  d. In spite of this, the system was to have no railroad crossings, traffic signals, or stop signs.

Answers and Explanations

Passage One

1. **a.** *Expertise* is the correct spelling.
2. **d.** The sentence is correct as written.
3. **b.** This statement does not help develop the argument about innovative road design.
4. **c.** *Limit* agrees in tense with lower and endanger.
5. **c.** *Built* agrees with the tense of have been.
6. **a.** Choice a is less wordy than the original sentence, but it retains the same meaning. Choice b doesn't use the first comma correctly. Choice c uses the semicolon incorrectly and thus creates a fragment in the first part of the sentence. Choice d changes the meaning of the sentence.

Passage Two

1. **a.** *Its* is possessive. *It's* means "it is."
2. **b.** *Humble* is the correct spelling.
3. **a.** Choices B, C, and D do not make sense.
4. **b.** Choice a leaves out the information in the fragment about the plastic lemon. Choice c changes the meaning of the sentence. Choice d uses the semicolon incorrectly.
5. **d.** Choice a uses a comma incorrectly. Choice b does not provide the correct tense. Choice c changes *delicious* from an adjective to an adverb.
6. **c.** The semicolon corrects the run-on while maintaining the connection between the ideas. Choice b is offers an incorrect use of the colon. Neither choice c nor choice d corrects the run-on.

Passage Three

1. **b.** *Tolls* is the correct spelling.
2. **a.** *Investments* is plural rather than possessive in this sentence.
3. **b.** The passage is not about current commuting patterns.
4. **d.** *Cities* is the correct spelling.
5. **d.** The sentence is correct as written.
6. **b.** This is the only change that maintains a logical idea meaning.

Notes

Notes

Notes

Notes